Family Matters So Does Business.

5 ways to keep your Family and Business Flying

2nd Edition

Pete O'Keeffe

Breakfree Forever Publishing

DISCLAIMER

 Author: PETE O'KEEFFE Title: Family Matters - So Does Business

Subtitle: 5 Ways to Keep Your Family and Business Flying

ISBN: 978-1916-030145
Category: Family/Business/Mindset/Goals @Breakfree Forever Publishing.

DEDICATION

To Ben, Michael, Claire, Louisa, Scott and Cynthia.

For all you have had to put up with as you have made your way in the world.

FOREWORD

Family Matters! So does Business can be read from start to finish in just a couple of reasonably substantial sittings. I like that about it. For busy people this book is not too time consuming, while at the same time it leaves you with plenty to ponder.

It may take a bit longer than a couple of sittings if you take notes and jot down any learnings as you go. I did a bit of this but in a very shorthand fashion. Alternatively, a bite-sized approach fits well, with the book broken into manageable and relatively self-sufficient sections.

Pete O'Keeffe delivers his thoughts in a conversational manner but with genuine conviction. It's personal and practical, including some nice quotes and stories to illuminate ideas or to demonstrate how to get started or how obstacles might be overcome.

As I sifted through the messages and ideas, I inevitably began questioning how well I manage my own balance between family and work? I don't think many, or any of us, get the perfect balance, but it certainly made me think a little more about what I prioritise.

I don't think Pete expects all aspects of the book to be embraced by the reader and the suggestion that quality time with family is not enough but that the quantity should also be prioritised is possibly too demanding for some people? The reality is that there is only so much time available but making the most of the time when sharing of a cup of tea or having dinner together can certainly help to stay connected and attentive to family members. I know with our kids the taxi service and chats in the car on the way to school or sporting events was another potential 'quality window'.

I'm also not a goal setter but I think that setting goals suits a lot of people. By writing down what's really important and having a vision it offers better clarity, as well as being helpful in staying motivated. The thoughts on goal setting were useful with regard to helping my kids as they try to work out what's most important to them and then having a plan to achieve those things.

In the drive for success, I think there's a balance. As Einstein suggested, "Try not to become a man of success, rather become a man of value", and that would certainly be a consideration for me when giving support and guidance to my kids.

The book is not a complete guide to finding your own balance, rather a collection of starting points and guidelines that can help the reader to construct their own framework for better communication and collaboration at home as well as in the work place.

With the plethora of life coaching books available, there is probably not one that is going to be the perfect fit, but reading Family Matters! So does Business offers a great opportunity for readers "to mine an ounce of gold" amongst the ideas proffered allowing them greater awareness and clarity about the way they plan, work and achieve what's really important in the home and in their business.

Joe Schmidt
Head Coach,
Ireland Rugby Football Union

CONTENTS

Acknowledgements 9

My Failure 11

Introduction 25

The Cockpit - Communication in Relationships and Business 43

#4 Engine - Mindset 65

#3 Engine - Relationships and Business 107

#2 Engine - Parenting Techniques and Business 167

#1 Engine - Goal Setting 185

The Landing - Final thoughts 223

The Black Dog 231

Appendix 245

ACKNOWLEDGEMENTS

I want to thank the following people for their inspiration and help in putting this book together:

Brett Odgers for pushing me to finally write down what has been a long journey that has been going round and round in my head.

Tim Rylatt for being such a good friend and inspiration.

John Alexander for allowing me to seek out his journalistic inspiration.

Matt Mills and **Simon Purcell**, my lifelong friends from Sacred Heart College. We have stuck by each other through tumultuous times in our lives, supported each other, and never judged one another.

Tosin Ogunusi for starting me off on my speaking journey and the idea of using the A380 as an analogy.

Jessen James, You called me 'selfish' when I was 4 days away from leaving the UK! Without you, I wouldn't be where I am today. Your intellectual candlepower would light up London if you were plugged into the National Grid.

Kate Muldoon and **Scott Frankland** for being on the journey with me as we write our books together.

My wife **Janelle** for being the glue that sticks me together, keeps me sane and who I love unconditionally.

Thank you.

I have taken inspiration and wisdom from these men and women whose books I have read. I have taken the liberty of using parts of their wisdom and including it in my book, and I acknowledge their wonderful ideas and thoughts. Your great ideas have inspired me and continue to do so as I keep journeying along my pathway.

50 secrets of persuasion
Noah J Goldstein, Steve J Martin Robert B Cialdini

The Minds of Winning Teams
Richard Maloney

Become a Key Person of Influence
Daniel Priestley

Lucky Legs: What I've Learned About Winning and Losing
Steve Gurney

Never Split the Difference: Negotiating as if your life depended on it
Chris Voss with Tahl Raz

ReWork: Change the Way You Work Forever
Jason Fried and David Heinemeier Hansson

The Definitive Book of Body Language: How to read others' attitudes by their gestures
Allan Pease and Barbara Pease

The Levels
Ray Moore

Think and Grow Rich
Napoleon Hill

Traction: Get a Grip of your Business
Gino Wickman

Turn that Ship Around: A True Story of Building Leaders by Breaking the Rules
L. David Marquet

Only Two Seats Left: The Incredible Contiki Story
John Anderson

My Failure

Realisation

I sat bolt upright, awake in my little hide in the bush. The night was as black as the inside of a 10-mile railway tunnel. It was 3:23 am, and the dial on my watch provided the only light around me. It was deathly quiet; nothing was moving; even the night owls were strangely silent.

My heart was thumping like a drum in my chest. Something wasn't right and the isolation of where I was continued to manifest itself in me. I suddenly realised the isolation I was feeling out here was the same isolation I felt in my marriage.

I was three days into an Outward Bound Course, a challenging outdoor adventure programme that is set up and run from a place called Anakiwa, at the top of the South Island in New Zealand.

It was the 'Solo' stage of the course, so I was by myself with little food and shelter. I had to make my own shelter and stretch my meagre food rations over three days. Being alone with nobody else anywhere near me, was the part of the programme where I had a chance to reflect on my life with no distractions.

It was during this time that a realisation dawned on me. My marriage was over. It was like a wave crashing over me; an explosion of foam and water that jostled me round as though I were in an agitador washing machine. I was getting crashed back and forth, up and down by my emotions.

Emotions that I had held in check for over 20 years were swirling around through my body. I held my hands over my head and tried to block these swirls of darkness. I quickly realised this was pointless. My life had led me to this point, and I had to make a decision. A decision I had tried not to think about for so long.

My heart beat louder and faster. This was not a great feeling, but as the wave of my emotions subsided, I started to get clarity. It was clear what I needed to do. These emotions had been pushed down for so long, and I hadn't dealt with them. I felt crushed.

At the same time, there was a glimmer of light appearing, guiding me toward a way forward. I looked up at the sky from my little hide.

I had been putting off the inevitable breakup for 20 years, but now I felt I had the courage and conviction to do something about it. I was popping the bubble. I was getting out of the washing machine. I was coming up from the depths of the swirling eddies of water.

Being by myself in the middle of nowhere, was the catalyst for my change. Out here, I was able to think and reflect on my life in a way I had never been able to before.

I had not paid enough attention to my family or my business and had abdicated responsibility for both. In the pitch dark and quiet, I realised I had made many mistakes. These mistakes had formed one huge rolling snowball that was heading downhill towards destruction at an extraordinarily fast pace. It had grown into a huge colossal unstoppable mass, thundering downhill, unable to be stopped until it hit something solid, or a decision was made, and then it would explode.

Everything I'd been working for all my life was about to come crashing down. I'd married young, worked hard and lived the script that was laid out for me. I had been pleasing other people and adhering to their values and requirements of me instead of my own. I had morphed into someone who wasn't me.

It made me shudder to think about what the fallout was going to look like. The 'snowball' had finally caught up with me because of my inability or inadequacy to deal with my issues. I had nobody to blame but myself.

As the reality of this started to hit me, I began to feel the weight of the decision I was about to make. An intense sadness weighed on me heavily as I sat alone in my hide. My whole body seemed to become locked down. My shoulders felt heavy. My breathing became laboured like a clunky steam engine. My legs felt like lead.

I cried. And I cried some more. Big rolling tears cascaded down my cheeks and dripped onto the carpet of bracken I'd been sleeping on.

Pictures formed in my mind. Pictures and images of broken men, fractured families and people I truly loved being totally devastated. It felt like a plane crash of epic proportions.

I had heard Outward Bound can provide life-changing experiences to its students. It did for me. Here I was out in the middle of the New Zealand bush, with only darkness surrounding me as I wrestled with this life-changing experience.

As I thought about it, I realised my wife was a wonderful, wonderful woman, and the most amazing mother to my three children. I could not ask for more. I had a lovely house, a property rental portfolio, a holiday home, and a successful business. Despite all this, I was empty inside and had been for such a long time.

I had wrestled with this issue before, but unfortunately, I had taken the easy way out for too long by doing nothing. Like many issues in my life, I didn't have the fortitude to do what was right at the time. I had let life happen to me by not controlling my destiny. I felt like a failure. I saw for the first time who I truly was. It wasn't a pretty sight, and I felt ashamed. Ashamed of myself for what I had let myself become.

Now, here I was, about to break the hearts of four people who didn't deserve what was going to happen to them.

At the same time, the business I had fought to build up over the years was in jeopardy. I wondered to myself, why I had not tried harder to keep both together. I realised it was the malaise that I had allowed to happen in my life because I wasn't in control.

The next few weeks and months were going to be tough. I was going to experience something I had never experienced before.

But, for the first time, I was on a journey that just might get me back to being the real me.

Have you ever held off on a decision that impacted on your life? After making the decision, did you realise that if you had made it earlier, instead of waiting, hoping the inevitable would go away, it would have had less impact on your life?

Would it have had a lesser impact on the people and loved ones that surround you, had you had the temerity to make the decision sooner? I call these 'The Taps in Life'.

Three Billy Goats Gruff

I thought about a popular children's story, The Three Billy Goats Gruff. My unhappiness in my marriage was like the Troll; it forever came up over the bridge to stop me passing into the happy pastureland. I had allowed it to happen.

I gave up trying to find the greener pastures because I was utterly exhausted. Everywhere always appeared greener, except where I was.

Being single again would be my bridge to redemption. I could get to know me again and reconnect with myself. If I could do that, I could identify my purpose, my values and my beliefs.

Looking back, I realise my whole being had affected my business because I never had the time to devote to it purposefully and properly. I didn't communicate properly, either personally or professionally. I had let myself down time and again, as well as those around me. It was time to sit still and find that happy place within me, instead of out there. I knew it was a journey that was going to be long and uncomfortable.

I had been on the hamster wheel for 20 years. I had tried and tried to get to the top but always ended up back at the bottom. I now understood why. I was in constant motion but going nowhere, looking for love outside of me instead of inside, where I should have been looking.

My journey now needed to be congruent with who I actually was. I couldn't let the toxic part of the break-up wash over me. The future would have many challenges, but I wasn't going to get paranoid about not being the best anymore. Trying to be the best at everything had consumed me, and it was not healthy. It showed my lack of self-esteem.

My family

My marriage had produced three incredible children, Claire, Michael and Ben. They had my height, but the rest of the good stuff, like their good looks, charm, intellect and personality, came from their Mum.

They did inherit my sporting ability, passed down from my parents. Their grandfather was an Irish national high-jump champion, and their grandmother was a national equestrian eventer.

Claire became a New Zealand National dance champion in Highland and Irish. Michael represented New Zealand at the 2012 Olympics as the goalkeeper for the football team. Ben became an international rugby referee and represented New Zealand at the rugby world cup in Japan in 2019.

They have also excelled in their respective careers, with Claire going on to be a top-flight PA in the mining industry in Australia, Michael a sports producer for TV sport, and Ben a Medical Doctor.

The beginning of the end

If I thought the Outward Bound experience was the only event that would change my life, I was wrong. The Molesworth ultra-marathon was another life-changing event.

The Molesworth is the largest sheep run in New Zealand; about 700,000 acres. Every year, on different dates, intrepid cyclists and runners, cycle and run through its interior.

At about 3000 feet above sea-level, the run takes you through 84km of barren, desolate landscape. The terrain is unforgiving on a dusty dirt road, full of potholes and ankle-breaking ruts. The air can be very still and dry; then within minutes, the weather can change into a raging torrent of rain, thrown down onto the land by massive rolling thunderclouds.

It was the ultra-marathon run day. I was in a team of four, and I was to run the second leg of 26km, the distance of a half marathon. Conditions for the run were hot, and the air was very still. A deadly combination for running at altitude.

We were about 2000 feet above sea level at this stage. I had cycled the same course the previous week in the cycling race and had recorded a very respectable time, obtaining a good place.

I was happy with my fitness, stamina and mental preparation. I was at my start position ready for the second leg. My teammate came in. We tagged, and I was off. I felt good.

After around 17km, something felt strange. I remember trying to drink water and fluids throughout the run, but I kept coughing them up. I didn't think much about it at the time, but it was to have dire consequences. I was dehydrating quickly, and I didn't realise.

I got to the 20km marker. I don't remember anything else until I woke up in the Doctor's surgery in a little town called Hanmer. I had literally run myself into the ground.

Apparently, I had collapsed on the road and had to be driven out to Hanmer to get medical attention. There were no medevacs there. They stabilised me and then sped me off to Christchurch Hospital. On the way, they had to stop twice to stabilise me. I spent five days in Intensive Care.

They told me I had Rhabdomyolysis. The body's Enzyme levels are meant to be at about 600; mine were at 4000. I was extremely sick.

The Doctors had thought I might not make it. They put me in the Coronary Care ward for five days. Other men around me were dying. It drove me nuts. I hated being around other patients who had given up.

During this enforced stay in hospital, I learnt a very valuable lesson about friendship and caring for people.

I had met Craig and Miranda Newbury through business, and they came to visit me in the hospital. I didn't expect them to come and I will never forget them taking time out of their valuable day to visit me and bring me a bar of chocolate.

The powerful lesson for me was that people do unexpected things at unexpected times. People come in and out of your life; some leave a lasting impression. I had made enough of an impression on Craig and Miranda for them to visit me. Their visit left a lasting impression on me. It maybe didn't have the same impact on them that it did on me for a variety of reasons.

Have you ever had an experience like that? An event that you remember profoundly, yet the other party involved would probably be left wondering what you were talking about?

This is the result we should strive for. Business and personal relationships should entwine, so people will go out of their way to help you or be there for you. The opposite should also be true.

This was the part I had never quite managed to get right; the quality of family and business combined. Craig and Miranda had shown me a sample of this.

I was going to ensure I didn't make the same mistake by separating family and business again. They somehow had to be interwoven together. I had to learn the secret of how to make this happen.

My learnings:

- [x] Family must come first; you can always start another business
- [x] Be congruent and true to yourself
- [x] Make decisions early, based on good information, mitigating risk, and being honest with yourself

The A380

INTRODUCTION

I have chosen the Airbus A380 as the perfect analogy for harmonising your family and your business. This aeroplane is one of the most complex machines ever devised by humans. Flying it takes a myriad of operations and checklists by the pilots.

Running a family or business is complex as well. Trying to run a family and a business at the same time is even more complex.

What can a family and business learn from an A380?

What is the relevance of using the A380 as an analogy to run your family and business? Let me explain, so you gain an understanding of the journey I want to take you on.

⇨ Airports must be specially equipped to handle the A380's 1.3-million-pound weight and 261-foot wingspan. They must widen runways and taxiways and strengthen their concrete hard-standings to accommodate its size and weight.

✓ *We must be specially equipped to run a business and a family at the same time. We need to understand the complexities of what it takes. Not every business owner is equipped to handle the challenges involved in successfully managing both.*

⇨ Authorities at Sydney Airport spent $AUS128 million to upgrade their infrastructure for the superjumbo jet's arrival. They adapted airport runways, the underground tunnels, and constructed special air bridges for the jet.

✓ *If you want to obtain the best for your family and from your business, you must recognise issues, change and adapt, in the same way as Sydney airport had to adapt for the A380.*

⇨ Each aircraft has more than 330 miles of wiring. If you laid all the wiring in an A380 end to end, it would stretch from Edinburgh to London.

✓ *Wiring is the communication element of our business and family. Without the proper wiring and communication, we can't run either properly. Communication and money are the two elements that cause most failures in business and marriages.*

⇨ Only 20 runways in the world are now fully capable of handling the A380 aircraft.

✓ *There are only so many partners in the world for us and only so many business ventures that we will be good at. We must pick the right ones. If we are marrying business and personal relationships together, it is even more paramount to choose carefully.*

⇨ The A380 has a cockpit and four giant engines to move it swiftly through the sky to its destination. These must work in unison to be effective.

✓ *In our business and family, the key is to manage all areas in unison to get the best result.*

This book will use five key areas to show you how to get the best from your relationship and your business.

The five key areas we are going to look at are:

1. The Cockpit - Communication in Relationships and Business
2. #4 Engine - Mindset
3. #3 Engine - Relationships and Business
4. #2 Engine - Parenting Techniques and Business
5. #1 Engine - Goal Setting

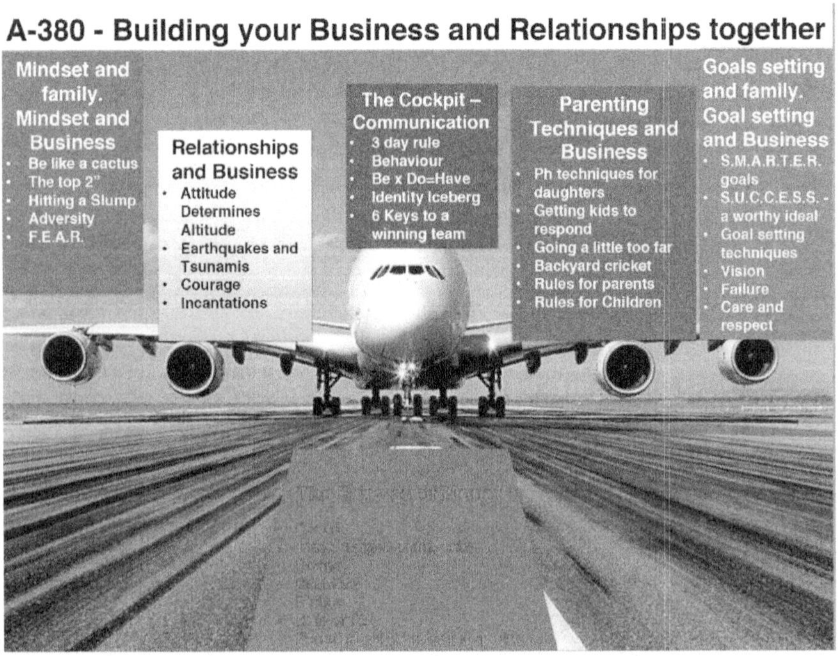

The goal of this book

Using the A380 as an analogy, this book offers guidance on how to be a successful business owner as well as being able to look after your family. To do this successfully takes commitment, time, and hard work.

My goal is to educate you, not to motivate you. A person who is motivated but not educated will just do stupid things faster! In business, you can't afford for that to happen.

I will help you debunk some of the myths about running a business and having great family time. The two can be done in harmony, but it takes congruency, commitment and desire. There is no instant-fix to get this right.

You will need to be pragmatic, persistent and resilient. Changes come from within. The changes people see on the outside manifest themselves through the learnings and implementation of good practice from your inside changes. The Identity Iceberg, which I will show you later, will help with understanding your outside and inside.

As we travel through these pages, I will share my successes and failures in getting these two areas right, my learnings and BFOs (Blinding Flashes of the Obvious.) I want you to learn from my mistakes, so you get it right.

The A380 poses challenges which not every airport is equipped to handle. Your business and your family will pose challenges as well, usually at the most unexpected times and inopportune moments. There will be turbulence as well as smooth air.

At the end of each section, I am going to let you know my three 'takeaway learnings' from what has happened. You should then take time to write in your learnings and the changes you want to make. Remember, it is up to you, and this is for you, nobody else. Only by taking ACTION, will the changes you desire be made.

Let's begin the journey. Let's start spooling up the engines.

5 Eggs and don't drop them

I remember doing a scenario in front of a business audience, where I asked for five volunteers. To each I gave a raw egg, still with its shell on. I let them know that each of them worked in a large corporation as an employee. One was the Sales manager, another the Operations manager, another the Marketing and Admin manager. Yet another was the HR manger and one was the Finance manager. These positions were their responsibility.

I said to them, "This egg represents your position in the organisation and what you have to do." I asked each to toss their egg up and down. Naturally they found this quite easy.

"It's easy, isn't it.? To which they replied "Yes."

I then said to the Sales manager, "You actually despise your bosses thinking they are not doing it correctly, and you believe you could do a far better job yourself. So you leave the company and become self-employed."

All of a sudden instead of juggling your Sales Managers egg, you now have to juggle the Marketing and Admin managers egg. With that the Marketing and Admin person gave him their egg. He was now juggling two eggs.

"But," I said, "You now have to be responsible for the finances for your new business as well." With that the finance person gave him their egg. He was now juggling 3 eggs – just.

"It doesn't stop here", I said, "You need to be able to handle the Operational side of the business as well as the HR side." With that the Operations and HR persons gave him their eggs. He now had five eggs he was trying to juggle – and couldn't. He started to drop one or two of the eggs, while trying to keep the others in the air. The dropped eggs, smashed on the floor at his feet. Looking down, he lost sight of the eggs we has juggling and dropped another one. Three eggs had now smashed. He wanted to stop, but I said no. "You wanted to start this business because you thought you could do a better job than your current bosses. Keep going"

"Stuff it," he said. "I want to go back to being employed." With that he threw the other two eggs on the ground and went and sat down.

And this is the reality of running a business, or a family. You are juggling all these balls, constantly. Trying to keep them in the air. You're juggling, time, juggling money or even juggling your ability to keep customers happy, or your children happy by taking them to their sports fixtures.

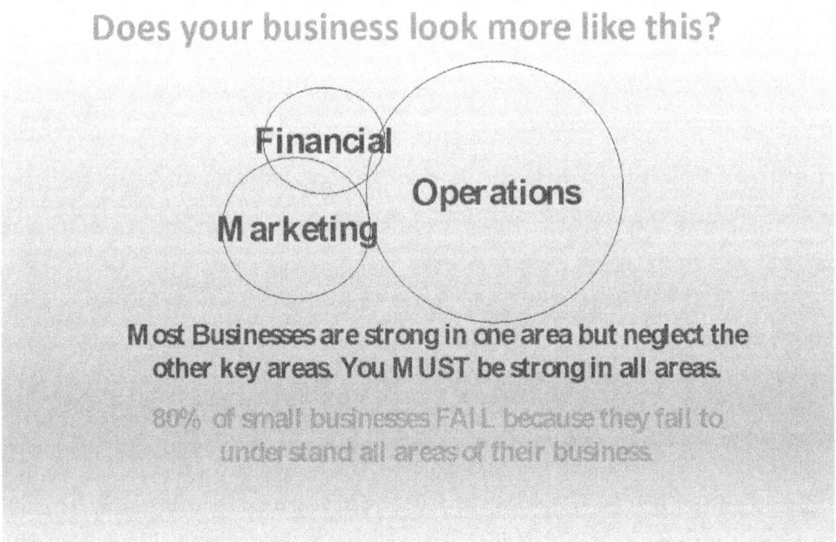

Most businesses look like this. A business owner is strong in one area, but the other 2 – 4 areas they will struggle with. As well as not understanding cashflow and cash-gap in the business for example, they are not strong enough in the other areas and don't spend enough time mastering them, or getting in the resources to cover their inadequacies. In fact 80% of all business failures is due to lack of understanding in the areas they are weak in. And they don't do anything about it to rectify the issue.

As a business owner you need to find that 'sweet-spot' and be strong in all areas. That means learning yourself, or bringing in the resources required to cover your inadequacies, so that it doesn't have an impact on your business.

There is no need to be a busy fool. Remember, you want your staff to be busy, not you. Or your business system to be busy, not you. That is why a systemised business sells for far more than a business that needs the business owner to remain in it until the new Business owner has extracted the knowledge from the previous business owners head.

When they buy a system (think McDonald's) they can dispense with you immediately as they have bought your system. They don't need to rely on what is in your head or you being in the business, as that has been extracted and systemised. This means you can sell your business for more multiples and remove yourself from the business. The new business owner has bought your system, not you, thus it is more valuable to him.

Interestingly. McDonald's has made more millionaires than any other business, or business system.

A question........?

What is more important, your family or your job/business?

Hopefully, your answer is family.

If family is more important, then why don't we manage family time and family finances with the same attention to detail and professionalism that we use in our job or business?

A story

I had started my own business. It was my first foray into being self-employed. It was exciting. I was going to be my own boss; I was going to make lots of money. I had bought into a financial franchise. At the time, I did not realise just how good the two franchisors were. They were incredibly helpful and gave of their time freely to help the franchisees have good businesses.

The first 18 months was hard, but I started to learn the ways of being a business owner. Looking back with hindsight, I was incredibly naïve.

The business was making money. I was enjoying a good lifestyle. I knew it would get better. I had employed two staff, and I was looking to open a new office in another county or province. Life was good.

I found premises in the new county (province) and employed another three people. More money started to roll in, but I was still working **IN** the business instead of working **ON** the business. I wasn't spending time teaching and training my staff. I wasn't being a particularly good 'boss.' I wasn't looking after my business or my family. I wasn't even looking after myself properly. I wasn't looking after the money. A fundamental concept I learnt early on; if you don't look after money, it won't look after you.

30 months in, and with two businesses going; the wheels fell off.

- The phone stopped ringing.
- I couldn't close sales.
- Staff started to leave.
- Money began to dwindle.

My P.A., sensing the down-turn asked if she should be looking for another job. I desperately wanted to say yes to save money, but I knew that things would be even worse if she left. I would have to take care of the administration and operational side of the business as well. I would be working longer hours IN the business and not working strategically ON the business to get us out of the current situation.

I applied for a job as an HR practitioner in another company and got it. It paid $NZ32,000 per year, a reasonable salary at that time, but not what I was used to.

I only had $NZ1000 in the bank account at this stage, and not enough money to go across to see the staff in my other business in the next county. The HR job seemed like a lifeline, a fix which I knew was only temporary. I wasn't looking long-term. I just wanted and needed money to keep the roof over our heads and food on the table.

The fear that gripped me was like a vice closing in around my chest. I couldn't breathe; my heart was constantly racing. I had a wife and three small children. I felt like I was failing. Days were long, and I didn't know what to do or how to close the business down.

I was not being a good husband or father due to the stress caused by what was going on. This was not an acceptable excuse for my behaviour. I had to manage this and change my behaviour.

One night I woke up at about 2 am and wondered what on earth I was doing. The HR position wasn't the answer; getting my mindset right was. I had to go back to doing what I had been doing previously and knew I could. I realised I had let many things slip.

The first task was to let my new employer know I wasn't taking the position. I did that the following morning.

I then went back to 'work.' I went back to work in my business!

I started to focus on rebuilding the business and my mindset. I asked my remaining employees for their help. Slowly the business turned around and evolved.

A year later, I was back on track, having learnt several valuable lessons.

- Focus on what is important
- Don't give up. It is not as bad as your mind makes it out to be
- Get that chimp off your shoulder. Get rid of his negative influence and be positive

I learnt: **I didn't have a money problem I had a focus issue.**

I was focused on the wrong outcomes.

Richard Maloney, the author of 'The Minds of Winning Teams', has this to say;

"There's just absolutely no balance to starting a business because your personal life suffers, your relationship suffers, your mental health suffers, everything suffers."

"Your finances go seriously down, to the point where you can be at rock-bottom. The key is you've got to be laser focused. You've got to watch for the warning signs. The warning signs are usually financial, asking you to go in a different direction."

"Most things stop because when you get major financial setbacks are you willing to just go through it? This is life telling you that actually there's a better route and if you've got the courage to keep looking around without your blinkers on, you'll find the way".

If your primary focus is 'instant gratification', then you will struggle to have financial freedom.

F.O.C.U.S. Is an Acronym for;

Follow One Course Until Successful.

F = Follow

O = One

C = Course

U = Until

S = Successful

Obtain focus so you know what to do. It's how you proceed from that start, that makes the difference. You need **PROCESSES** to help you keep that focus. If you think differently and **focus on your goals**, you'll be prosperous. It's a long-term change and a process. It is not an event.

Events are short-term changes. That's why people who win the lottery can be destitute again within a year or so. It is an event and not a long-term strategy that gave them riches. Processes are for a long-term strategy.

Most people can't understand how to focus because they have never been shown what to do or how to do it. When you are taught **how to focus on what is important to you** and where you can end up by following a **process strategy, then you will be successful**. Concentrate on your focus, and you will do well.

So how do you change? Please understand, we are not looking for massive change. Start with small consistent changes.

1. Start with affirmations. Self-affirmations to yourself, every hour, every day until they become a habit. Think positive thoughts. I talk more about the Top 2 inches later. I have put an affirmation sheet at the end of this book for you to help you start your own.
2. Reach out and get a coach or mentor. Someone who you respect and has run a successful business themselves. Someone who will hold you accountable to do what you say you will. Someone who won't let you off. Most importantly, someone you can confide in and talk to, who you can be vulnerable with, and to.
3. Set your goals. At a minimum, one personal and one business. Write them down. Use pictures when you write them. Our mind works in pictures, not words. Start with the end in mind and work backwards. Make sure your goals are S.M.A.R.T.E.R. I'll talk more about S.M.A.R.T.E.R goals later. Let's at present just use an example.

   Goal: To have a net profit of $50,000 per year from my business by (date). Current net profit is $20,000, so I need to earn another $30,000. Let's assume your goal to achieve this in 5 years' time. Therefore you need to earn on average another $6,000 per year to reach the extra $30,000, which gives you a net profit of the $50,000 you desire. Let's break this down further. $6,000 per year is $500 per month, or approximately $115 per week. It seems far easier to achieve $115 per week, or $500 per month, than striving for $6,000 per year. Would you agree? This goal is specific, measurable, achievable, relevant and time bound. Lastly you need to attach some emotion and reward to it. So the goal is now:

Goal: To have a net profit of $50,000 per year from my business by (date). When I achieve this, it means my business is successful, and I have the money to do the annual family holidays I dream of. I will reward myself by having a small family holiday every year when the annual milestone is reached, and in 5 years I will reward myself by taking the family overseas to…

4. These 4 small changes will change the way your life is and what and how you achieve. Often we try to over-complicate life. Keep it as simple as you can and let technology take over the complicate parts of life when you can.

My learnings:

- [x] Commitment and desire are keys to moving forward in any endeavour you undertake
- [x] Change is constant. If you're not growing, you're dying
- [x] Have a system so your business is not reliant on you

Your learnings:

- [ ]
- [ ]
- [ ]

The Cockpit

Communication in Relationships and Business

True communication is the response you get.

Communication

The cockpit is the heart of the A380. Two Pilots with a myriad of instruments to watch, monitor and assess, must communicate, physically and verbally to ensure the smooth progress of the flight.

The safety of nearly 500 passengers seated behind them, is in the way they communicate. Trusting those two pilots to deliver them safely and on time to their destination, is what passengers pay money for.

Communication between pilots, cabin crew and passengers, ensures a smooth and uneventful flight. We need appropriate communication when we fly, and we need it in our business and in our family.

Communication has a ripple effect across all facets of our business life and family life. When we start at the epi-centre we do not know what the consequences are, that communication can have on people. We do not know how far our communication ripples out into other people's lives – for good or for worse. Sometimes we have no control over that.

It's important that we understand just how important communication is, both in Business and family life.

Think of communication like this.

You have a chicken, and on your way to town from your farm, you pluck out a feather from the chicken on every step you take as you walk along, and toss it away. Some are big feathers, some are small downy feathers. Finally when you get to town you have plucked all the feathers from the chicken. (Yes the chicken is probably cold, but this isn't the point of the exercise!!!!)

Now turn around and walk back to your farm and along the way, pick up all the chicken feathers you have plucked.

Of course you can't. Some of the feathers have been picked up by other people, not necessarily friends. Some feathers have been picked up by friends. Some have been blown away in the wind. Some even are floating away down the nearby river. Some have been trampled and broken, or run over by cars.

The moral is that once you have communicated something, it is very hard to retrieve. So think carefully every time you communicate, whether it be verbal, written, a signal or even a hand or facial gesture. Your communication can be misinterpreted. And especially if there is emotion attached to any communication.

In the building industry they have a saying, "measure twice, cut once." With communication, think twice before you say or send out your communication.

Rebuilding

I was living by myself. I had sold the business and was receiving an unemployment benefit of $NZ190 a week. My rent was $NZ160 per week, leaving me with $30 for power, food, petrol and anything else I needed. I was borrowing money from any source I could find, just to stay afloat.

It's amazing when, at times like these, someone comes into your life that will completely change the direction.

Some believe this is the Power of the Universe; I believe my God was at work. He had quite fairly punished me for my wrong-doing, but he was also there when the changes in my life were happening. When I wanted to make good changes, he gave me another chance.

I had known Janelle for several years. We had been in the Marlborough Property Investors Association together. She came back into my life as a friend and helped me out of my desperate financial situation. She also had three children from a previous marriage. As I got to know her, I found there was more to this woman than I realised.

Janelle played such a significant role in my learning and the foundations for this book.

To keep a relationship and business together requires the ultimate demonstration of communication, skill, love and accountability. It requires consummate skill, continued application and knowledge.

When the vestiges of romance and excitement wear off, and the cycle of life, children, work, responsibilities and financial issues rotate day after day, month after month, year after year, it takes a special person with a special ability to work through that and keep the love and romantic fire still kindled and burning. Janelle opened the door and showed me this.

I had to learn this for myself, and I had to ask for help. In the past, I had been too arrogant to seek help. As I lay in my hideout in the bush on my Outward Bound course, this realisation dawned on me hours before the sun rose.

The Future belongs to the Askers. It was time for me to ask and seek help.

A story

My wife and I were going away for the weekend. My son, Ben, wanted to borrow our second car so he could impress someone he was dating.

"Yes, you may borrow the car," I told him, "as long as you mow the lawns first. Is that a fair deal?" Ben pondered on this said he thought that was fair and agreed to the terms.

We came home from a lovely weekend away, relaxed and happy. Meeting us at the door was one very grumpy son.

"Dad, you never left the car keys for me," griped Ben. "My whole weekend was ruined".

"Funny," I said to him, "I'm sure I tied the car keys onto the lawnmower handle before I left. Shall we go and check?"

We often talk about the importance of communication without actually giving it the attention it requires. How many times have you been introduced to someone only to forget their name seconds later? Communication is as much about **listening** as it is talking. In fact, it is twice as important; hence we have two ears and one mouth.

Your relationship and your business are based on communication; listening and talking, usually in that order. At the core of anything that happens (or doesn't happen), is how you communicate that desire. Not only the verbal communication but your tonal communication and your body language as well. We read a lot into people when we view their body language.

This is why we start with communication. Get this right, and it makes the job of understanding your relationship and your business needs so much easier.

People like to talk about themselves and their lives and tell you their thoughts and opinions. Never be afraid to ask questions and be a good listener.

In fact, by listening and allowing another person to talk about themselves, you will never be short of an audience.

Handwritten notes

One of my Mum's regular sayings was, "**manners maketh the man.**" I'm sure this was passed on from her father to her.

Manners were one of several "non-negotiables" that Mum instilled into me as being incredibly important.

She taught me the art of handwriting thankyou notes, cards and letters. I absolutely hated the aftermath of birthdays and Christmas because I knew the pen and paper would come out. I would be expected to write 10-15 thankyou cards or letters to people who had given me a gift.

My selfish tendencies were apparent. I liked receiving the gift; I just didn't want to write letters to say thanks.

"Why can't I just say thanks next time I see them?" I would say to Mum. This never got me anywhere.

Nowadays, with instant email and text messages, it's easy to say thank you. However, it doesn't have the same weight attached to it as a handwritten expression of thanks. This is one discipline instilled in me for which I will be eternally grateful to my Mum. I now realise the power of the written word.

Often, I go to friends' houses or a client's place of work and see my handwritten letter or card from a previous occasion, still sitting on their shelf, sometimes months after I have written and sent it to them.

The power of the written thank you note is there for everyone to see. It reminds the owner that someone cared enough to take time from their day to write and thank them for something they have done.

It shows that you have taken the time to think of them and personally write to them to express your thought. In your own handwriting, that thought, expressed on paper, is ten times more powerful than any email or text message. Your handwriting doesn't have to be perfect or written neatly. Try it and see for yourself what happens when you personally write a thank you note to someone. I guarantee you will be blown away by the response you receive.

Unresolved issues

Many hostile arguments result from unresolved issues which fester below the surface for days, weeks or sometimes months at a time. They later explode because of some innocuous comment.

Have you ever tried to have a firm argument with someone, only for them to blind-side you by bringing up some small infraction from weeks, months or years ago? You have no idea what they are talking about or how to respond.

You wonder where that explosion came from; it seems totally out of proportion to what you said or asked. You are taken aback. Is this really the issue, or is there something else underneath the surface that has started this?

What started as something small, has now manifested itself into something far bigger than the original issue. However, the anger belongs to something said or done long before this discussion.

The 3-day rule

Janelle and I came up with the '3-day rule' which we put into practice pretty early in our marriage.

It came about because one day I was acting the fool and annoying Janelle, just a little. Suddenly, she exploded, and told me I was 'being silly', and to 'stop acting like a school child.' With that, Janelle stormed out of the house, slamming the door just about off its hinges on the way out. She jumped into the car and roared off in a cloud of rubber and smoke. Where did that come from, I wondered. It was out of all proportion to what I had been doing or saying, or so I thought. I was a little perplexed.

Later that day, we sat down with a glass of wine and talked about what had occurred. Janelle said that my little instances of goading her had finally come to a head on this day and she had exploded out of all proportion to the incident. Wow, I thought. That's interesting.

I hadn't realised my behaviour was having such a dramatic impact. I wonder what may have transpired if we had talked about the issue when it first happened instead of a few months later. We then decided to instigate our 3-day rule.

The 3-day rule states:

Anything that needs to be said, discussed or resolved, must be addressed within three days of the initial infraction. If it is not, then it is not deemed important enough and must be forever disregarded, never to be brought up in conversation again.

This rule allows a frustrated partner to say:

"I would like to talk with you now about an issue that is bugging me."

or

"I am really angry right now; please give me a couple of hours to cool off, and then let's talk".

Each party knows it is important, but it takes the heat out of the situation.

Now the objective is to explain what the issue or behaviour is that is causing the problem. Personal attacks or jibes have no place in the discussion.

Saying something like, "You are really annoying, especially when you interrupt me," is not specific and can cause the argument to get personal. The other party could respond with, "Well you really annoy me too," and the discussion quickly degenerates. What is it that is annoying?

An effective way to have the discussion goes something like this;

"Thanks for taking the time to talk with me. I want to let you know that I was frustrated when all the dishes were left on the bench for me to pick up and wash after I had cooked dinner. It was frustrating to have to do it all. May I have your help to ensure we keep the kitchen clean and tidy, and we help each other?"

The other party can see their behaviour was not appropriate, and most importantly, there is nothing personal in what has been said.

It means that issues are resolved quickly and within a defined timeframe. It does take a little getting used to, especially if you are one of those people who is used to bottling issues and not dealing with them in a timely fashion.

The problem with bottling issues is that when the bottle is shaken, the fizz starts to bubble, and your cap explodes. Issues you didn't want to address in the heat of the moment are raised with emotion. You communicate less effectively than if you were in a rational state of mind. It becomes ugly, and there is a culture of blame. Anger overrules the sensitivities of each person, and hurtful things are said. One party wants to win at the expense of the other. Rarely does this strategy work for a harmonious relationship.

The 3-day rule allows for issues to be spoken about and resolved in a timely and respectful way. Both parties know what the issues are that you are talking about and resolving.

When both parties are committed to the 3-day rule, it shows a mark of maturity and respect for each other and the relationship. Once resolved, the issues don't need to be brought up again. Both parties can move on.

The 3-day rule in business

The 3-day rule can be used in business in the same way as within your family. Try it. You'll be amazed at the impact it has on other directors, colleagues or employees.

When used properly, people in the business feel respected and valued. Gossip and backhanded sniping cannot fester. All issues are out in the open and resolved within 3 days. It allows for transparency and shows a work ethic that thrives on open and honest communication, regardless of how hard it may be.

"I would like to talk with you now about an issue that is bugging me."

or

"I am really angry right now, please give me two hours to cool off, and then let's talk.

The effective way to have the discussion will be something like this;

"Thanks for taking the time to talk with me. I want to let you know that I was frustrated when I was talking with our client, and you interrupted the conversation. I was frustrated because the sale was nearly complete, and the interruption could have jeopardised it. I wonder if next time we can discuss our strategy before the client comes in, so we know what each other is expecting."

This is about behaviour and not about personality. The other party doesn't feel 'attacked' and can understand your perspective.

It will take time to implement and must be led from the top. The boss must display the right behaviour and show the team they are committed to the 3-day rule by applying it whenever the opportunity arises. It takes a commitment from the other party as well, regardless of where they sit on the organisational chart.

When behaviours are discussed, and nothing said is personal, it allows for clear dialogue and an ability to discuss the problem and the behaviour and to resolve the behaviour that is causing the issue.

Mistakes will be made when implementing the 3-day rule. You won't get it right every time, but if you're committed to making the change, you will get it right more times than not, and that leads to a more harmonious relationship or business workplace.

Be committed to it, and it will happen; you'll be surprised at how quickly any perceived disputes or slights can be resolved.

Communication is like a light bulb. You depend on power from another source. Unless you stay connected to someone you trust, you will be spiritually weak. Connect with your partner, so the light burns brightly. Connect with your work colleagues, so you are all more productive and focused.

Behaviour is so important that we use it in our Business with clients. Richard Maloney taught me how to implement Behavioural change with clients through his excellent Engage and Grow employee programme.

If you have 5 or more employees in your business and you want growth and stability, then I thoroughly recommend this programme.

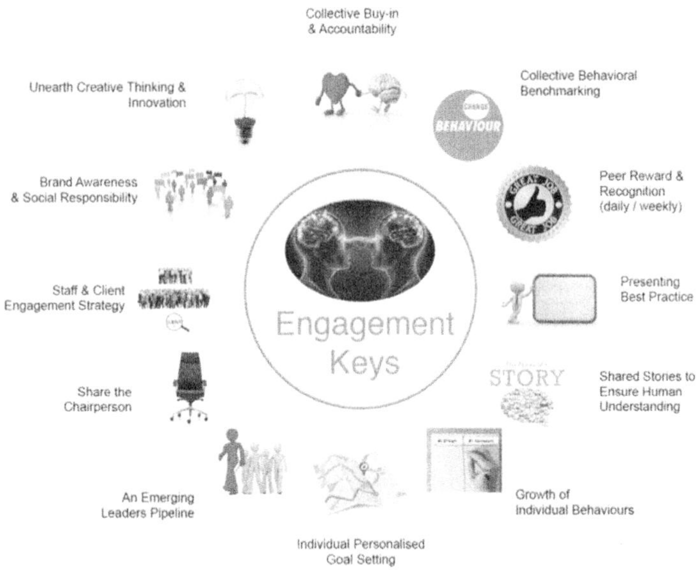

All of the keys in any programme are bespoke to that particular business and ensure behavioural change, proper communication and accountability. To give you an example, let's look at Key 2: Collective Behavioural Bench-marking. All participants must come up with 5 collective behaviours they want to see implemented into the business. Each week thereafter, one participant at random is asked to name those 5 behaviours. The team then give examples of these behaviours they have seen in the business over the previous week. This attached to other keys, of for example, 'Story-Telling' and 'Emerging Leaders Pipeline' brings about profound positive behavioural and communication changes within the business.

Like pilots in the cockpit of the A380, all business owners and staff are all heading to the same destination and wanting the same positive outcome.

It is the same with family.

TO THE SEA! TO THE SEA!
TO THE SEA! TO THE SEA!
BRRR!! TOO COLD!
TO THE BAR! TO THE BAR!

One last thought on Communication:

With the advent of e-mails, texting, messenger, or the other myriad of social platforms available for us to communicate on, it is easy to have what you say, misconstrued, or even worse to send a communication by these forms while you're emotional or angry.

Please never reply to any correspondence while your angry. It's too easy to write it and send, and then later regret what has been sent when the emotion has evaporated.

In our Grandparents day, because letters look time to write, the emotion was usually diffused before they sent the correspondence. These days it is so easy to fire off a response in 'the heat of the moment' and then later regret it.

NEVER send a response when emotional. Write the response by all means as this is cathartic. Don't send it though. Leave it and walk away from it. Come back to it a few hours later and re-read it. If you're still happy with your response then send it. If not reword it and then send it. Or give it to someone else to read first before you send it and be guided by their response to you

My learnings:

- ☑ Everyone loves a handwritten thank you note sent to them. It doesn't matter if they are a business associate or a friend
- ☑ Communication is like a lightbulb; turn it on to get results
- ☑ The 3-day rule ensures issues are dealt with quickly and effectively

Your learnings:

- ☐
- ☐
- ☐

Communication: Behaviour v Personal

When General Robert E. Lee was asked by Confederate President Jefferson Davis to give his opinion about a particular officer, he gave a glowing report.

One of the officers in attendance was amazed at his words and said to Lee; "General, do you know that the man of whom you speak so highly of to the President is one of your bitterest enemies and never misses an opportunity to criticise you?"

Lee said; "Yes but the President asked my opinion of him. He didn't ask for his opinion of me".

It takes character, compassion and courage to speak well of a critic but when you do, three good things happen:

1. You increase your value. You show you're able to rise above criticism by bestowing praise on another.
2. You defuse your enemy's criticism of you. When people hear your praise of a critic and their disdain for you, their respect for you rises, and they see you in a different light.
3. People see you as fair-minded and generous. It takes minimal effort to strike back at a critic, but it takes great character to turn the other cheek and bless them.

How many fights or wars began as a result of someone taking a slight or offence at something that was said that they felt aggrieved at, or that they took in the wrong vein?

It's not personal

Allan Pease, the body language expert, says communication is broken down into three areas:

7% - the words we say

38% - the tone we use

55% - our body language

It stuns me how little impact our words have in a conversation compared to the tone of our voice, or the body language we exhibit.

While words can sting, you must be mindful of the other two powerful influencers in the communication triangle.

You must understand that often people are talking about your behaviour and the way you act. This is entirely different from what they think of you personally.

I often used to take things people said about me personally. One that really floored me, and made me realise how far I have come, was when a colleague said to me that I was "evangelical and not very pragmatic". I bristled with indignation at this comment. I took it as a personal affront.

I asked him to explain, because I have always thought of myself as pretty pragmatic. I was then going to argue my case right back at him.

He said to me that I am so busy trying to help others before I get my own house in order, that I am not particularly pragmatic.

I sat back and thought about this. This was about my behaviour. I took this as a real compliment. Five years before this, nobody would have called me evangelical.

It made me realise how much my behaviour had changed. It's nice to know that even in times of trouble, I am now trying to look after others, as opposed to just thinking of myself and my troubles. I have become a better person.

The crux of this is to look at your behaviour. Are you exhibiting the correct standards in your personal and business life?

Is your behaviour congruent with what you are saying and what your actions are showing? In business and relationships, we often get into a malaise of just 'doing.' You need to understand the 'being'.

My learnings:

- [x] Ensure when I communicate, it is about a person's behaviour; don't get personal
- [x] I am in this world to make a difference
- [x] Words have far less influence on communication than tone and body language

Your learnings:

- [ ]
- [ ]
- [ ]

#4 Engine - Mindset

At take-off, the A380's four Trent 900 engines will deliver a thrust equal to the power of more than 3,500 family cars. The engine fan operates at nearly 3,000 rpm with tip speeds at 1.5 times the speed of sound.

Every business needs power and movement to deliver the energy required to get it going. Speed and attitude are paramount to getting the business to a stage where it is ready to take off.

Depression

My depression started after my fall during the Molesworth run; I just didn't recognise it at first. It affected me immensely and came to prominence about the time I was on my Outward Bound course.

I was trying to function as a normal human being, trying to run the business. I knew I was driving myself into the ground but couldn't understand why. I was not looking after my family or communicating properly.

After I returned from Outward Bound, I left the marital home. A while later, I sold the business. It was an awful time for everyone involved.

On reflection, I was arrogant. I needed a bit of that in the business to make decisions, but I wasn't a nice person with it. I believe I was quite manipulative and Machiavellian in my outlook.

These are the things I had to learn to temper and change. Not only for my own good but also if I wanted to run another business successfully or to have another close relationship.

I needed to learn from my failures, then take these apart, learn and rebuild . I had to change. Otherwise, I would just deliver the same result.

If someone new came into my personal life again, I needed to be ready with a 'new me'. If I was to have another business, I had to be a 'new me'.

A story about mindset

At the Battle of Agincourt, the British were outnumbered by the French army five to one. In a legendary stroke of genius, King Henry delivered a motivational speech that would live on for centuries.

He said; "We few, we happy few, we band of brothers..."

But what was equally brilliant is that in addition to the motivation, he had a tangible and real physical plan, a procedure to accompany the motivation. It was called the "long bow".

The French mounted their giant steeds, clipped on their knighted armour and thundered across the field to engage the band of British bowmen.

Henry had his men wait and wait and wait as the charging onslaught got closer and closer and closer. The fear of the British bowmen became greater and greater as the horses neared.

At the last critical moment, Henry had his men unleash a mighty volley of arrows across the field, then another and another. The French fell in multitudes. The day of armoured knights came to an abrupt end on the field at Agincourt.

Technology and motivation had won the day.

Technology and motivation had won the battle.

I love this story because, in business and life, it is not enough to only have motivation. You have to have a physical process to be executed as well.

In business, life, and our relationships, having a plan is critical. Having the right mindset to achieve that plan is also critical.

Before the A380 takes off on its journey to its next destination, the pilots file a flight plan, so they, and air traffic control, know where they're going, the track they will take, and at what time they should arrive. Like King Henry's plan to use the long bow, the pilots have a plan to get to the next destination as quickly and as efficiently as possible.

We live in both a physical and metaphysical (nonphysical) world. They have to co-exist. It's one thing to be motivated, but you don't want to be motivated and not educated, otherwise, you will simply do sillier things faster.

Use motivation and the correct process to generate sales, income and results. Use motivation to ensure you are looking after your relationship. Have a process that looks after you and your partner. Remember, you can inspire others, but only they can motivate themselves. You can't do it for them.

What is the executable physical process that goes with the inspiration?

Inspiration without a process in a result-oriented world will ultimately leave you confused, over-hyped and cynical.

Process without inspiration has little meaning and will result in substandard performance and burnout. Process without inspiration leads to separation and divorce within our family unit.

Like Henry, you have to have the motivation, education and inspiration, as well as the physical application to 'ground' the learning. Like Henry's men, you have to be patient and resilient. Don't run in the face of opposition; trust that your process will work.

Why is patience necessary? Because motivation moves at the speed of thought and generates an instant sensation. This is why you can do sillier things faster with only motivation.

A physical application takes more time to execute and is, therefore, slower to experience. Most people pull out before they give a strategy time to develop.

Moral to the story

If you don't have the sales, income, emotional or physical results that you want, or you don't have the relationship you want, then one of the elements is missing.

You have to be grounded in both worlds, physical and metaphysical. If you want to create great results, apply what you learn immediately, even if you make mistakes. Your mindset is important.

Attitude determines altitude

In the scheme of mindset, your attitude determines altitude. When David and Goliath came head to head, the Israelites said; "*He is too big to bring down*".

David's mindset and attitude were different. He believed in himself and said; "*He is too big to miss*," and focused on bringing Goliath down.

Attitude has a lot to do with your success and your ability to get what you want.

Remember, your capacity to achieve exceeds your current level of performance.

If you want to rise to the top in your current employment, invest one hour every day in learning more about yourself and your industry. Developing this single habit can make you an expert within five years.

Success is the continuous pursuit of knowledge. If you want a successful business, do the same. Invest an hour every day in learning more about yourself and your business. This habit allows you to have a strong and healthy business. You are in control.

Why would we invest an hour a day into our business, without doing the same for our relationship or marriage? This habit allows you to have a strong and healthy relationship with your partner. Often, we have the wrong set of priorities.

As a leader, you are called upon to make decisions regarding relationships, money, time, values, opportunities and disputes. Your decisions show up on the bottom line. In that realm, it takes longer to recognise your brilliance or your stupidity because you're forced to lead for long periods of time without the benefit of knowing whether you made the right call. By the time your crop starts coming in, it's too late to change your 'agricultural procedure'.

Earthquakes, tsunamis and attitude

After the Indonesian earthquake in 2008, a group of businessmen said; "*We have been through this before, and we will rebuild. We have had SAR's, we have had the Bali bombings and now this. We will rebuild our island and our businesses.*"

Imagine the strong mind and will of these men as they see this havoc and destruction all around them but still have the vision of a better future. That takes resolve, a determined mindset and a spirit of self-belief. I imagine that if we spoke with these same businessmen in two years' time, they would once again have thriving businesses, but they will also be prepared for the next event.

Every business owner has their good times and their tough times. Vision is the ability to see ahead and rebuild.

Every marriage or partnership has the good and the rough in the relationship. In both scenarios, you must see through the rough, knowing that rebuilding can and should happen in every instance when there seems no hope. Your mindset is one of your most powerful attributes to forge through to the next stage.

Be like a cactus

A cactus never dies, no matter how difficult the environment or the terrain. The cactus will outlive anything else in the desert, through sheer grit and determination. Our self-talk or mindset determines our success and what opportunities we embrace. You should have a mindset that is like a cactus. Never give up and never die. You may be a minute away from success without realising it; if you give up, you'll never know.

What are you worried about?

- 40% of the things we worry about never happen
- 30% are in the past and can't be helped
- 12% involve the affairs of others that are not our business
- 10% relate to sickness, real or imagined
- Only 8% of things we worry about are likely to happen

The top 2 inches

The top 2 inches of our head determine our destiny. I spoke about this at the beginning of the book. The top 2 inches is our subconscious mind; what and how we think. Fill your subconscious with powerful, positive thoughts, and it will go to work making them happen for you.

As you read this book, you are reading in the fore-conscious. It is the here and now. It is immediate. Your fore-conscious helps you know right from wrong. You can pick aspects from this book that you agree or disagree with.

The subconscious (top 2 inches) works 24/7. It doesn't know right from wrong, so it goes to work to make the dominant thought in your mind happen.

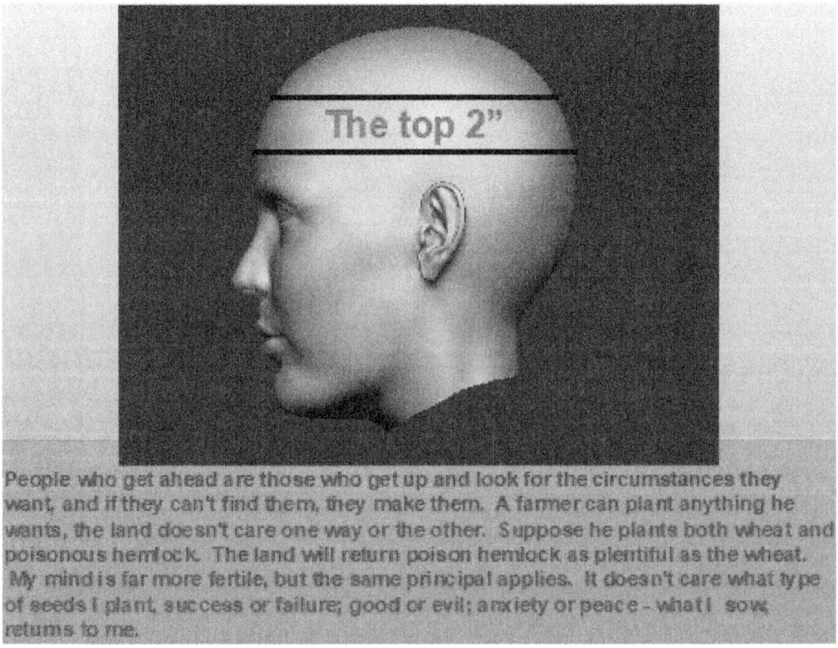

If that dominant thought is negative, your subconscious will help make that happen. Have you ever heard someone say; "I'm always late", and they are? It's because they have put being late as their dominant thought. Their sub-conscious helps them make being late, happen.

Elite athletes visualise their race before they run it or visualise their game before they play it. They are putting positive dominant thoughts into their subconscious, and no doubt they have been putting those thoughts into their mind for weeks or months before the event.

The subconscious is the future and works when the fore-conscious has stopped or gone to sleep.

If you fill your mind with powerful and positive thoughts, then your top 2 inches realises this must be important (even if it is not true) and it will go to work to make it happen for you.

As an example, you say; "I am making £7,000 per month income within 2 years". It may not be true at this immediate time but filling your mind with this thought will make it happen. You must be positive. You can't have negative goals. Your mind can't work in negatives.

Have you ever woken up in the middle of the night, with an answer to a problem you have been mulling over for a while? You wonder how it came about. That is your subconscious at work, getting you an answer to the problem you have been concentrating on and thinking about. This is because your sub-conscious realises it is important to you.

Tip: *When this happens, write down your thoughts immediately. Otherwise, when you wake up again in the morning, you will have forgotten the answer your subconscious worked so hard to provide to you. I always have a pad and pencil by my bedside for these answers that come to me in the middle of the night.*

Use a pencil, because in the dark you can still write upside down so you don't have to turn on the light or disturb your partner. A pen, upside down quickly runs out of ink, due to gravity!

Because your sub-conscious has provided the answer you have been seeking, it will now forget it. That is why it is so important to write it down 'in the moment', because when you re-awake in the morning, you will have forgotten the answer your sub-conscious has worked so hard to give you.

I've always understood how powerful the mind is. People can 'will' themselves into dying because the doctor told them they only had six months to live. Conversely, they can live an active life for another 10 or 20 years because they refused to believe or give in to the doctor's diagnosis.

Focus

We have traversed FOCUS already so take your focus and the goal you want to achieve, and look at it before you go to bed. Let your subconscious work it over during the night. Don't focus on weaknesses, focus on strengths and make them better. Don't have a lot of strong weaknesses.

Form the habit of letting your subconscious work for you. A habit is something you do so often it becomes easy. Your habits will determine your future. Until you clearly understand what is holding you back, it is difficult to create more productive habits. The only pre-requisite is that you must commit to change. Listen to motivational audio books or recordings when out driving, walking or exercising. This is a habit almost all successful people have developed.

Commit to making decisions. Swap; "Let's think about it" for; "Let's decide on it". Don't wait for perfect solutions. Decide, then move forward.

General George Patton, during the Second World War, implemented the maxim, "*An average plan violently executed now, is better than the perfect plan implemented in a week's time.*"

Fashion will always fade away. When you focus your mindset on **permanent** features, you're in bed with things that never go out of style.

A story

I had wanted to get the latest Jaguar XE Turbo R-sport. I liked the car and I 'wanted' it. I cut a picture of it out of a magazine and placed it on the wall beside my bed. I saw the picture when I went to bed, and I saw it when I woke up in the morning. The picture was also in the colour of the car I wanted.

I set a time frame; I was going to have the car in nine months' time. I talked about it with my wife. I looked when I saw other Jaguars driving along the road.

My top 2 inches realised I wanted this car. I started to dream about it.

Guess what happened nine months later? I couldn't get the car.

I refocused and said; "I'll have that car in three months' time". I worked hard to make my dream happen. My top 2 inches was buzzing with the thought of the car.

Guess what happened? In three months', time. I got the car.

It was amazing to drive; I loved it. I had realised my dream, and it was great. It was only my timeframe that was wrong. That's something my top 2 inches couldn't help me with. What it did help with was to focus on getting my dream car.

Now let me explain something. I missed getting the car in the first 9 months. Does that mean my goal was wrong? No. My timing was out, so I reframed my timing and 3 months later, I got the car. Don't give up if your goal isn't achieved in the timeframe you have set. The goal is right, the timeframe may not be – so don't give up. It just means something wasn't quite in tune or all the parts to make the goal happen weren't available.

How to change the mindset

I want to share with you, one of the most profound lessons I have learnt in life. This changed me and the expectations I placed on myself. It's called the **Identity Iceberg.** It comes from the mindset formula: Be x Do = Have

Like all icebergs, 90% is under the water; you only see the top 10%, above the waterline. We judge ourselves based on the environment we exist in, as do others.

Be (under the water)	x *Do* (above the water)	= *Have* (above the water)
Be	x Do	= Have
Our Thoughts	Our Actions	Results
What we be	Who we are What people see	What we do What we achieve
Skills) What Beliefs) people Values) don't Identity)see of us	Behaviours) what people see Actions)of us and judge Decisions) us on	

Environment

What surrounds us

- physical (clothes you wear, car you drive, house you live in)
- people (do they build you up or pull you down?)
- knowledge (books we read, videos we watch)

Do

'Do' is the <u>10% of the iceberg you see above the waterline</u>.

The 10% people see is made up of your

- behaviours
- actions
- decisions

They see what you do in the world, how you act, and who you are. You get judged on these things without a person knowing what is going on with you under the waterline.

Often you hear people say; "don't judge me on how I look, judge me for who I am inside". Unfortunately, this is easier said than done.

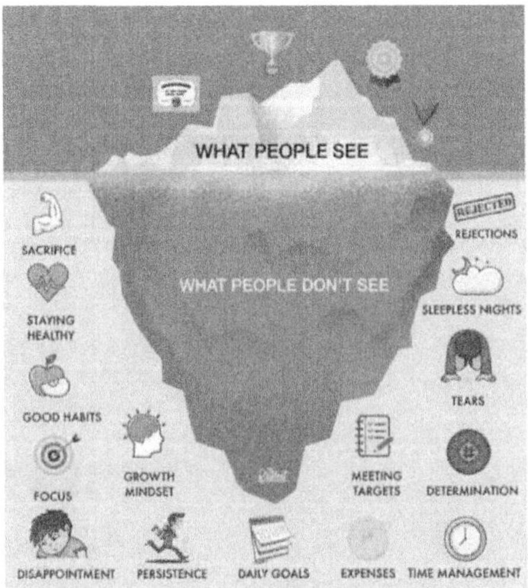

Before anyone can get to know your **BE**ing, they see your exterior; your **DO.** How you dress, how you act, the body language you display. All these external attributes determine whether a person wants to know you better, or whether they are put off by your appearance. You may be the most wonderful, beautiful person on the inside, but if your appearance puts someone off before they get to know you, then it is a lost opportunity.

In business, people make up their mind about us within seven seconds of meeting us. Your appearance needs to be congruent with who you are.

Be

'Be' is the 90% of the iceberg under the waterline. The most important part of any change in our behaviour is our '**Be**'.

Under the waterline are our

- skill level
- beliefs
- values
- identity

The deeper you go, the harder it is to change.

Skills can change constantly, that is why you have the capacity to change jobs or change direction in your business. Your education continues after you leave school because you won't do something if you haven't developed the skill.

Beliefs are something you hold to be true right now. For most people, their belief system now is usually different from the beliefs they held even a year ago. As you grow up through your teenage years, your beliefs are constantly changing due to your environment.

In business, your belief system changes as you get more adept at managing your business. This sometimes impacts on your family because your belief system is rooted in the fact that if you just work a little harder, the rewards will come and then you can cut back. The issue here is that you are now forming a work habit of overwork; the continuation of constant work takes over to the detriment of your family and personal life.

Values are the rules by which you live your life, and these are deep-seated. They start very early in life and come from watching and interacting with our parents, our siblings or friends during our schooling and trade or university life. You take these values into your business. Very rarely do you change values unless you have a profound change in your life.

Identity is one of the hardest and deepest parts of us to change. Our identity is deep-seated from a young age, and you only change when you have empirical evidence to support that change. Going to war, for example, would create a profound change in your identity because of what you see, hear and feel in that war-zone.

Our environment

Our skills, beliefs, values and identity are encapsulated in three areas:

1. The **people** you spend time with. Surround yourself with people who build you up, not tear you down. Run as fast as you can away from people who have a negative influence on you. If they are family, then spend as little time with them as possible.
2. Your **physical** environment. The clothes you wear, the house you live in, the car you drive, all tell people something about who you are as a person.

3. The **knowledge** you seek. The books you read, the videos you watch or the newspapers you read

You need to believe three things:

- You are in this world to make a difference
- What separates a great business from any other, is the people. It is the people in companies that make them great.

  What separates a great relationship from any other, is the people in it and how hard they are prepared to work to make a good relationship into a great one.
- You cannot get anywhere unless you know two things
  - Where you are now
  - Where you are trying to get to

My learnings:

- [x] I must be like a cactus – a cactus never gives up
- [x] Only 8% of the things I worry about will happen
- [x] My 'BE' is the most important part of me to get right

Your learnings:

- [ ]
- [ ]
- [ ]

YOU WANT A WHAT!

Hitting a slump

Remember the story I told you about me working in my business for about 30 months, when I hit a huge slump? Just about everyone I was talking with didn't want to buy my product or service anymore. I couldn't understand why. I was flummoxed. The product and service was the same, my script was the same, I was the same, or so I thought. And here was the learning.

When I look back, I realise there had been a little shift in who I was, and how I was doing my trade. I had stopped doing some of the fundamentals in my business that had made me successful. It was a very gradual shift. It wasn't blindingly obvious, and that is how it crept in slowly under cover with me thinking I was still doing it the same. Luckily, I caught it early enough before it did really serious damage to my business. It was still a slump though.

One of the main reasons for a stoppage in results is that you're not practising the fundamentals. You can work your way out of it with the right mindset. Results are at the top of the iceberg and should be visible. However, it is the 90% under the water, your **BE**, that you must change to achieve the results you want.

You can always get more money, but you can never get back time.

You can always have another partner, but not the same relationship.

You can always start another business, but not have the same results.

Life is full of cycles. They don't last forever so take things a day at a time. Focus on the results you want. Develop the mindset to obtain these results and **BE** prepared to pay the price to get there.

The A380 has been developed from a series of previous aircraft designs and thought processes. The belief was there from the Engineers and Designers to make it happen. But the skills or knowledge to develop such a large aircraft were not available a decade ago. Neither was the technology. Time has allowed technology to catch up and develop such an aircraft.

It is the same with your business and relationship. Take the time to develop your skill and your mindset. Take the time to develop your knowledge and understanding of who you must be to ensure a great business and a vibrant relationship. If you want to rise to the top, invest one hour every day in learning more about yourself and your industry. Developing this single habit can make you an expert within five years.

To be effective in the outside world, you need:

- A strong sense of moral purpose
- An understanding of the dynamics of change
- An emotional intelligence as you build relationships
- A commitment to developing and sharing new knowledge
- A capacity for coherence making (enough coherence on the edge of chaos to still be creative)

This too shall pass

Nothing lasts forever. Time has a habit of pushing us through the good times and through the bad times as well.

A saying I live my life by is; "**This too shall pass**."

When life is going well, I'm prepared; "**This too shall pass**" (**darn it**)

When life is a struggle, I'm prepared; "**This too shall pass**" (**thank goodness**)

When you constantly put your life in the "**Have-to**" position you put yourself under pressure. When you live your life from a position of "**Choose-to**", you are in a position of power.

Decide to shift your focus. Decide to shift your mindset.

Make every activity a conscious choice. When you constantly make better choices, you create better habits. Better habits produce better character. When you have better character, you add more value to the world. Remember, your dominant thoughts (top 2 inches) usually win out when it comes to everyday decisions. Success takes effort and consistent focused activity.

Quality of Life Ladder

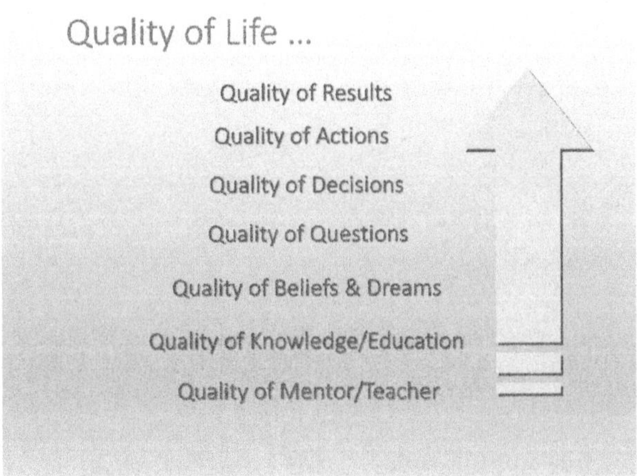

When the pilots are flying the A380, they have had expert training in the aircraft systems and how it flies. They have trained for every conceivable emergency that could happen.

The quality of their mentor or teacher, allows them to have quality knowledge and education of the aircraft. This, in turn, gives them real belief in their training and what they do as they fly the aircraft

Remember Qantas QF32 that had to land back at Singapore after one of its engines blew up en-route to Sydney and ripped off part of the wing? Those pilots had real belief that they could land the plane even with the huge amount of damage done to it. They realised that by skill and good training they would be able to land the aircraft and have only 139 metres of spare runway at the end, after the roll-out. Wow, that took skill and belief to make that happen. And they did it because they asked each other quality questions to ensure they made quality decisions, which in turn lead to quality actions, which turned into a great result where nobody died.

If you apply the same Life Ladder to your business as the A380 pilots do, then:

- The quality of your mentor/coach helps you determine the quality of knowledge/education you gain to run your business
- This allows you to have a better belief system and dreams for what you want to achieve
- This leads to a better quality of questions you ask yourself in your business
- Which helps in your decision-making to make better quality decisions as opposed to rash ones

- This helps you take better actions for the business and understanding the ramifications of those actions
- Which in turn now gives you great results.

Use this same formula in your personal life as well, so you make good decisions and get great results for you, your partner and your family. Having a family mentor or coach is equally, if not more important than a business coach.

Acquire knowledge for application toward a worthwhile end. University degrees do not guarantee successful careers. If you seek additional knowledge, first determine the purpose for which you want to gain the knowledge you are seeking.

If you want to rise to the top, invest one hour every day in learning more about yourself and your industry. Developing this single habit can make you an expert within five years.

Adversity

One of the main weaknesses of humanity is the average person's familiarity with the word impossible. Nobody is ever defeated until defeat has been accepted as a reality. Every adversity that you have, brings with it a seed of an equivalent advantage. Look for it, and you will see it. Keep your mind closed and you will miss another opportunity.

Millions of people believe themselves 'doomed' to poverty and failure because they believe they have no control. In many cases, they are the creators of their own misfortune because of their negative belief, which is picked up by the subconscious. They are unable to work through the Quality of Life ladder to great results.

Impossible by using the same words but adding an apostrophe and a space can change the whole dynamic of the word from Impossible to:

I'm Possible.

A story

Louisa my step-daughter went through the adversity triangle when she was applying for a full rowing scholarship to West Virginia University in the USA. She had seen Michael persevere and succeed at Fairfield University in Connecticut, USA. She decided she wanted to obtain a University scholarship to the USA as well.

Her journey was tough, and she had to overcome so many roadblocks and obstacles as she journeyed to her destination of a full scholarship. She was tenacious in her resolve to push through. Instead of lumping all the roadblocks together, she took each one individually and broke it down to its component parts and then worked on it and then overcame it. She then moved on to the next one until she had beaten every last one and was admitted to the University on a full rowing scholarship.

As Louisa went through this cycle, she learnt from Michael to have positive affirmations. She wrote down and affirmed her positive thoughts and behaviours at least twice a day, but sometimes more if she was struggling.

Louisa realised her subconscious didn't know right from wrong. She realised her subconscious mind would act only upon thoughts she gave it that have been mixed with emotion or feeling. So, she got her subconscious to go to work for her. She gave it the positive information it needed to help her. She gave it good stuff in positive thoughts, positive affirmations and it went to work to churn out a good answer for her. And that is exactly what happened.

Claire also used positive affirmations when she was studying and practising for her NZ Highland dancing exams. This was a long, arduous process and her Mum and I often heard Claire reciting her positive mantras as she studied and practised. Claire told me once that it put her into a higher state of consciousness, and a higher state of excitement when she recited her positive affirmations.

Claire now teaches dance and has set up a specialised dance studio in her home in Perth where she teaches dance. All around her studio, are affirmations that she now teaches to the next generation of students.

Professionals have coaches; amateurs do not

Choose your friends and mentors wisely. Look at all professional sports teams or sports people. They all have coaches in their corner, mentoring and guiding them. Why would we not want that for our business or our relationship?

Be careful from whom you take advice. Most people ask advice from people who are financially illiterate and up to their eyeballs in debt.

Why do people stay where they are?

F.E.A.R.

F.E.A.R. is an acronym for

False

Expectations

Appearing

Real

People fear many things; growing old, being in a car crash, losing money. Sometimes the fear they feel is irrational.

FEAR is just interest paid on trouble before it comes due.

For example, the fear of flying. You would have to fly every day for 19,000 years before the probability of being in a plane crash approached 100%.

It is a mistake to suppose people succeed only through success. They often succeed through fear and failures. And you're not defeated until the past takes your focus off the future. Don't fear failure.

Failure is not failure unless you let it become so.

Failure or a mistake is just a learning opportunity to understand what went wrong and how to correct it for next time. When Thomas Edison was developing the light bulb, he had 10,000 failures before he perfected it. However, he never once said he had failed; he believed he had just found 9,000 ways that a light bulb wouldn't work. How many of us, would have given up after 100 failures?

Often the difference between a hero and a coward is that a hero hangs in there five minutes longer.

When you run from intimidating situations, fear multiplies until eventually it controls your life. But when you tackle your problems head-on, your confidence rises until you reach a point where you're no longer controlled by fear.

You have to be willing to get back up and keep moving forward. It takes tenacity to keep persevering after you've done your best and before you've seen results.

Look at Abraham Lincoln, now revered as one of the greatest American presidents. This is what he went through and overcame to get to where and what he wanted:

- 1832 defeated in state legislature
- 1833 failed in business
- 1835 sweetheart died
- 1836 nervous breakdown
- 1838 defeated for Illinois house speaker
- 1843 defeated in nomination for Congress

- 1854 defeated in US Senate
- 1856 defeated in nomination for Vice President
- 1858 defeated in US Senate race

A story about Abraham Lincoln

During the American Civil War, Lincoln signed an order transferring certain regiments. Secretary of War, Edwin Stanton, refused to execute it, calling the president a fool. When Lincoln heard, he replied; "*If Stanton said I'm a fool, then I must be, for he's nearly always right and he says what he thinks. I'll step over and see for myself*".

He did, and when Stanton convinced him the order was in error, Lincoln quietly withdrew it.

Part of Lincoln's greatness lay in his ability to rise above pettiness, ego and sensitivity to other people's opinions. He wasn't easily offended. Nor did he fear being wrong. He welcomed criticism and in doing so, demonstrated one of the strengths of a truly great person: humility.

FEAR

Four enemies you will have to clear out before being successful:

- Indecision
- Worry
- Doubt
- Fear of failure

Indecision is the seedling of fear. Fear is nothing more than a state of mind. Fear of poverty is a state of mind, nothing else. If you want riches, you must refuse to accept any circumstances that lead toward poverty.

Worry is a state of mind based upon fear. Worry is a form of sustained fear caused by indecision. Most individuals lack the willpower to reach decisions promptly and stand by them.

Keep your mind closed to all people who depress or discourage you in any way. Seek people who influence you to think and act for yourself. Successful people have successful habits. Take time off to think about your goals, your business or family.

A story

Before my eldest son, Ben left for University to study for his medical degree, he couldn't make up his mind whether he would play rugby at University or give it up due to the intense study he had to do, especially in his first year. Indecision was weighing him down.

I suggested he should look at becoming a rugby referee. It would mean he could still be part of the game, without the worry of injury through tackles. In fact, he would probably have the best seat in the house for any game.

I had been a reasonable referee, getting up to provincial level, so I knew what opportunities existed. If Ben was any good and he refereed up the levels, then the NZ Rugby Union would fly him around the country to referee various games. It meant he could have time out from study and academia.

Ben thought and pondered on this for a little while, and being his own man, made the decision when he got to University. He is now a top-flight international referee, and this came about from indecision back in 2008. Ben formed good habits in the decision-making process.

I know some people who take half a day a week just to think. This will give you unusual clarity, especially if times are tough. Thinking positively about your future and planning to do something about it, will help you succeed. Most importantly, you will learn more about life and your capacity to succeed when you are uncomfortable.

Often, when your back is up against the wall of fear, the greatest breakthroughs occur.

Most of the time, fear only exists in our minds. Our imagination is powerful. Step into your fear. Unfinished business is an on-going reality. Every week, something happens that needs to be resolved. Don't allow things to fester. Everything you want is on the other side of fear. To overcome fear, you must have faith in the outcome. Confidence is required at the height of your fear.

Stop **doubting** yourself and get on with positive initiatives.

One of my greatest fears when setting up my first business was my fear of running out of money. I let this fear manifest itself, and eventually, it started to happen. Because I was thinking about it, my subconscious went to work to 'help me' make it happen. Realising this, I changed my thought patterns and thought about the abundance of money that I needed, and it was about then that my universe changed. Thinking good powerful positive thoughts and affirmations about having money changed the direction of my business.

One of the most common causes of failure is the habit of quitting when one is overtaken by temporary defeat. Everyone is guilty of this mistake at one time or another. Failure is a trickster, with a keen sense of irony and cunning. It takes great delight in tripping one up when success is almost within reach.

The **Fear of failure** is endemic in us all, from time to time. A previous bad experience is 80% of the reason why people don't buy. Fear of rejection is 80% of the reason why salespeople don't sell.

Go to the mirror and look at yourself. It is not everyone else's judgement that counts but what you see in the mirror. This is the verdict that matters. This is the person to please. You've passed the most difficult test if the person in the glass is your friend. If you've fooled the world but cheated the person in the glass, you'll still end up with tears.

A thought

Like a turtle, you have to stick your head out of your shell to move forward. Don't let **FEAR** inhibit your actions or your desire to achieve. To be successful you need to overcome your fear of being rejected, and to stop worrying about what other people will say about you.

Don't get caught up with **FOWOPTOM** = "Fear Of What Other People Think Of Me". Turn the thought around; "*What you think of me is none of my business. What is most important is what I think about myself*".

The boundaries of a person's reality often do not change until that person forsakes what they feel comfortable with and goes blindly with faith.

My learnings:

- [x] F.E.A.R. is only in my mind
- [x] I must remember "This too shall Pass" for positive and negative events in my life
- [x] 7 quality questions determine my life

Your learnings:

- [ ]
- [ ]
- [ ]

The formula for change:

There are many Formulas for change and how to overcome the fear of change. Two that I find most useful are:

I x V = R

Imagination mixed with **V**ividness becomes **R**eality.

and

(D x V) + FS > R

(**D**issatisfaction x **V**ision) + **F**irst **S**teps must be greater than any **R**esistance for change to happen

The mind thinks in pictures, not words. Think about what you dream about. You never see the word 'Ferrari' in your dreams. You see the actual car. You picture its colour. (And I bet you're now picturing a red Ferrari!)You see yourself driving it. What we vividly picture in our minds and desire, will become a reality. Plan how to achieve the goal you want.

I was at a workshop recently when I used the Ferrari analogy, and before I had completed the sentence about thinking in pictures, one of the workshop participants yelled out "Red!" I laughed as it so vividly demonstrated the power of thinking in pictures. He saw his Ferrari in the colour Red. It's an iconic colour for a Ferrari. The power of what he did, demonstrated to all the other participants how we all thought in pictures.

What are you dissatisfied with?

What needs to change in your business and your family life?

What is the Vision you have for that change?

What are the First Steps needed to make it happen?

If your Resistance to these changes is greater than the change you want, then you will never change. Here's how the formula works to see if you will change. Score yourself out of 10

(D	x	V)	+	FS	>	R
7		8		9		5
7	x	8 = 56	+	9 = 65	>	5 x 10 = 50

Therefore 65 > 50, so you will change

(D	x	V)	+	FS	>	R
4		6		3		7
4	x	6 = 24	+	3 = 27	>	7 x 10 = 70

Therefore 27 is not > 70, so there will be no change. And more importantly, you will be resistant to that change

A paragraph I observe from my bible reads; *'Put off your former conduct and be renewed in the spirit of your mind.' Ephesians 4:22-23.*

You must correct your Mindset so that you think positively for the correct outcome. Mindsets are patterns whereby your mind automatically operates in a certain way. That means you can set yourself up for misery by reacting to the same people and circumstances, in the same way, yet expecting different results.

Maybe you are saying;

"After all these years, I thought he'd change."

"How come I'm the only one who makes an effort to stay in touch?"

It's easy to blame your problems on others;

"Look what he's doing."

"Look how long I've waited."

"Why doesn't she call?"

We think the answer lies in getting the other person to do what we want, but that kind of thinking is self-defeating; it gives control to others. Your happiness isn't determined by other people, even if you've convinced yourself it is.

An experienced counsellor writes; "*If you don't like the same results, try pushing a different button. Are you waiting for something to change, instead of doing something different? Stop pushing the same button and ask for clarity to see the situation honestly and to act with wisdom and responsibility*".

John Anderson in his excellent book, 'Only 2 seats left' explains that your brand (next to your health) is the most valuable asset you have.

People move on or change, but a brand is always there. Some brands are so powerful they don't need words; for example, Boeing, Coca-Cola, McDonalds and Apple.

Let's look at how powerful your name is. It is one of the sweetest sounds you will ever hear when someone calls your name or asks your name. It is personal and specific to you.

Your name is about integrity, honesty, credibility and reputation. This refers to your business as well. Always protect your name, enhance your name and never let any damage come to your name or your business. Always honour it and treasure it.

Why do brands last a lifetime?

- Quality
- Consistency
- Innovation
- Value for money
- Trust – this is the most important of all

A quality brand means you can charge what the market will bear for your product. Your name means you can charge more for your service if your name implies honesty, help, integrity and an enhanced reputation.

The Line Of Success.

Every day you have a choice. You can play above the line or below the line. I call this the Line of Success.

When you play below the line, you are in B.E.D. That is, you blame others for what is happening to you. You use excuses for not achieving and you are like the river in Egypt – in Denial.

When you're below the line, you are looking at the past, you're default response is 'why me' and you play the victim. You're like a hippopotamus wallowing in mud. You look for reasons for failure.

Conversely when you play above this line, you are using an O.A.R. An oar can move you forward, sideways and even backwards to be able to move forward again.

When you play above this line, you take Responsibility for your actions, you are accountable for what happens and you take ownership of the results. It's your Own Ship. Here you are future looking. You ask 'how' questions to get you to your destination faster and you play the winners game. Results drive your forward like a strong pull on the Oar.

The Line of Success

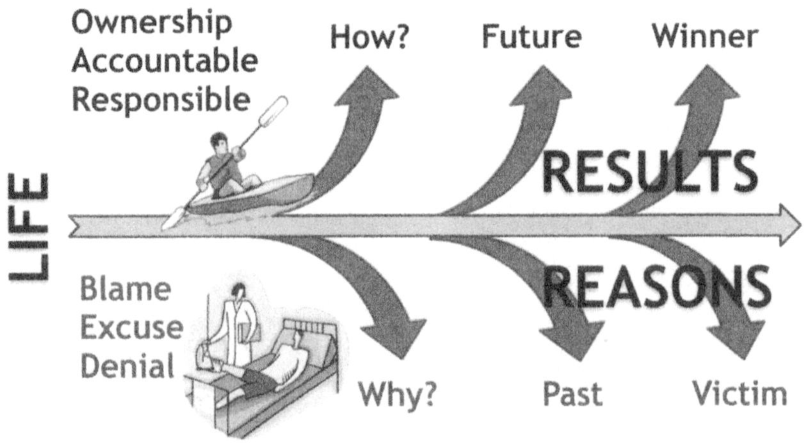

You have a strong mindset and you have a strong desire to achieve. Setbacks are temporary and a small blip in the way of you getting to your destination. A strong mind is a pre-requisite to playing the Line of Success.

Some formulas to put into practice in mindset

I'd never had the formula to strengthen my mindset until I came across **P.A.N.E.**

A friend of mine Tosin Ogunnusi showed me this formula, along with several others. His website can be found at the end of the book.

What does it mean?

- **P**rivate dialogue
- **A**ssumptions
- **N**ature
- **E**mpowerment

Private dialogue: the conversations in my head.

Your state determines the quality of your decisions.

If you're in a negative state, then you'll make negative decisions

Real thinking takes a conscious effort to always think good thoughts. Go back to the Top 2 inches again and the Quality of Life ladder.

Assumptions: what beliefs from my past have I allowed to inhibit me?

- What has it cost me?
- What have I missed out on?
- What will happen if I keep these negative beliefs?

Nature: what is my connection and how do I communicate to myself and others?

Empowerment: I must deal with the power of my intention.

Steve Gurney in his book 'Lucky Legs', describes it perfectly;

"Energy flows, where attention goes."

"Thinking is the power to get me to where I want to be."

Focus absolutely on the positives in your life and business, and the positive outcomes you want and desire.

You have to put in the work to do what you want to do and be who you want to be. Again: **Be x Do = Have**. The work of changing your 'Be' to realise your 'Do' will give you the 'Have' and the Results you desire.

Get a new belief, a positive belief, - and actually believe it.

What do you intend to achieve and commit to? You can be world class if you let yourself be. What is the strategy needed to become world class?

Empower your mindset with new beliefs. Your partner and your business will thank you for it.

Think about your Line of Success. How often do you play below that line, staying in B.E.D., when you should be pulling on that O.A.R. If you're in B.E.D., get out of it immediately and find your O.A.R.

We gave our children the opportunity to be world class. They then had the choice to believe they could, or just be mediocre. It makes me proud to see them all achieving at such high levels, but it took belief, tenacity and perseverance to get there.

Incantation sheet: My New Identity

I have always been a strong believer in affirmations but found that one-liners such as; "I am a strong coach," or "I am going to have a great day," never really worked for me. I would put them up on my wall, but I quickly lost interest in them.

I met Tosin Ogunnusi in 2016 and participated in one of his workshops. There were 23 of us on the course. Tosin described how he affirmed to himself every day and showed us his incantation sheet. I was mesmerised. This is what I had been looking for. It resonated with me, allowing me to put in place the words, actions and inspiration that defined who I was, and who I wanted to be.

I have included this incantation sheet in the appendix with instructions on how to create your new identity. I hope you find it as inspiring as I did.

My learnings:

- [x] A High Performing Team is paramount in any business for it to succeed
- [x] I must use the formula for change. Impossible actually means I'm Possible.
- [x] Energy flows where attention goes, so I must play above the Line of Success

Your learnings:

- [ ]
- [ ]
- [ ]

#3 Engine - Relationships and Business

The A380 provides us with a superb example of relationships and how to make them work. In the early days of flight, the captain was a God, and all in the cockpit deferred to him. This resulted in some incredibly bad decision-making or no decision-making at all, which in turn led to crashes. They weren't accidents, because it couldn't be described as an accident if nobody was communicating.

As crashes happened, investigators found a disturbing parallel. If there were no real relationships between pilots and engineers, regardless of seniority, then there would be a break-down of cockpit management and communication. This would lead to fatal errors or missed instrument malfunctions during the flight. Relationships are fundamental in the cockpit, just as they are in business and family.

Getting back on the bike

Adversities that come along to bury us usually have within them the potential to benefit us. Pick up the pieces that come from the adversity and ensure a new benefit tumbles out of the learning. The world isn't going to stop and wait.

It's like falling off a bike during a race; the race won't stop and wait for me. I must get back on the bike and start pedalling flat out to catch-up. (Only in the Tour de France do they stop and wait for the lead rider if he falls.) I wasn't in the Tour de France. I was on a far more important personal journey.

With my failure in my marriage, I realised I needed to have the fortitude to pick up myself and my bike, climb back on the saddle, and start cranking the pedals.

I was starting my journey of life again...........

A story

I was working with a very successful business owner who I'm going to call 'Steve'.

Steve had all the money in the business to do pretty much whatever he wanted. Time was an issue for him, an issue he didn't want to address, but his family did. He was oblivious to their needs and desires.

He had four beautiful children but didn't spend much time with them. Instead, Steve worked to get the money to purchase 'items' for them.

Next week would be the time for family he would say to himself. He would just finish this next job and then it would be OK. But the 'next week' never came. There was always just one more thing to do.

Another issue for Steve was that never took time for himself to reflect on what we was doing, or where he was going, both spiritually and as a man and a father and husband.

I asked him once, "Steve, when was the last time you actually sat down and reflected on where you're going and where your life is leading you to?" He looked at me blankly, as I thought he might. Time to, and for, himself was something he didn't factor into his life.

Steve was often away with friends on golf trips or watching some sporting event in another country. Any form of sport was worth watching but following F1 was a real passion.

Steve came home from one of these breaks to be confronted by his wife. She delivered an ultimatum to him. Stop the boys' trips and spend more time with the family or else.

Steve dismissed what he heard from his wife as an idle threat and went back to work. Having just returned from a trip, work was fun because his colleagues wanted to hear what he had got up to.

Business was good, and the money was still rolling in. He told himself that in the next six months, he would step back from work and start to spend time with the family. They had everything that his money could buy, so he thought they would be pretty happy.

A few months later a friend called and said he was off to the Italian Grand Prix; he wanted to know if Steve would like to come along. It was a two-week trip.

Steve consulted his calendar. There wasn't much in the diary. He had worked to get to this place of having a "*commercially profitable business that could work without him*", just as I had suggested. His GM could look after the business in his absence.

He rang me to let me know he couldn't make the next coaching session. I asked him what his wife thought about this trip. I was aware of the tension within the family. Steve was quite dismissive; she would get over it, he said, she had before. Before he left on the trip I asked him to reflect on what he was doing and just exactly where he was in his families priorities. I left it to him to decide.

Steve had a great trip away and even got into the pit-lane on two of the racing days. He was ecstatic. It was all over social media.

He and his three friends also got to have a holiday around Sicily. It was a place he had always wanted to visit after reading 'The Godfather'.

When Steve came home, he found his house empty. The furniture was there, but his family wasn't.

Steve wasn't too worried. He thought they must have gone away on holiday without telling him. He'd always let his family know when he was going away, so he thought it was a bit rude of them not to tell him.

The next day he went into work and found his team very subdued. He wondered what was wrong with them. He asked, but everyone was very coy.

Finally, his GM took him aside and had a quiet chat with him. The business was being closed down. His wife had taken the extraordinary step of hiring a legal team to get her half of the business. This had been going on for about six months, and Steve wasn't even aware.

He sat there stunned. He didn't understand why his wife would do such a thing. After all, he had always been the provider.

Steve rang me to work out what he should do. I let him know he needed legal advice, not coaching advice. He also needed communication advice. He had the template for this. It had been five of our coaching sessions. I suggested he go and re-read it.

To his credit, he did, and he had a huge **BFO – Blinding Flash of the Obvious.** It had been there all along, waiting for him to open his mind and be aware of what was around him.

Steve started to eat 'humble-pie' and acknowledge his deficiencies. He spoke with his wife and children and acknowledged to them that he had been a selfish idiot. He recognised that he had put himself and his lifestyle ahead of the family and realised how stupid he had been.

He realised also, he had been so busy, being busy, that he hadn't taken time for himself to reflect on how his life was changing incrementally ever so slowing, but without him knowing, seeing or realising it, until it was nearly too late.

Steve and his wife started to go to couples counselling. He realised the importance of his family and what he was nearly losing.

Slowly the relationship with his wife and children started to mend. He returned to coaching, and we worked on his delegation and communication skills. He spent less time at the office and more time with the family. He went to his children's sporting events. He took an interest in what they were doing at school and their progress. He now understood and became very proud of what they were achieving and how his wife had kept all this together while he had been away being an idiot.

He took time to reflect on himself as a person and what changes he needed to make personally.

The business continues to run without Steve being there full-time. He spends as much time with his family as possible now. He now works with a local charity, helping them as well.

Steve is happier now than I have ever seen him. He realises the importance of family and how he nearly lost everything, and now he uses the business to fund his lifestyle with his family.

Work allows and gives you the ability to enjoy the personal lifestyle you want. Too many business owners have this the wrong way round, They live to work instead of working to live.

You have gone into business as a means to an end. To have a choice. To have a better lifestyle. To be your own boss. Not to work all the hours of the day and then come home hungry and tired, grumpy with the kids, and not acknowledging your partner. Forgetting to even ask about their day but expecting them to cater to your every whim because you've had a hard day.

Does this resonate? If it does, it is time to start changing. Now.

Connect with your partner and family. Work will always be there; family won't. The kids grow up and move out of home. They are entrusted to you for such a short time. Don't waste the opportunity.

Stop saying; "*Next week, I'll take time off to be with the family*".

Next week never comes. All of a sudden, you wonder where the kids are, or why you don't have a relationship with them anymore. Or, you come home and find your partner has had enough and has moved on.

Me Time:

Let me open another can of worms, that was nearly Steve's downfall. What Joe Schmidt taught me as "<u>Me time</u>". It's about having time for ourselves.

While I talk about the whole-hearted commitment to family and to business, the ability for an individual to have time to themselves these days, and to regenerate and to reflect is missing? This is such an important element to grasp because we have so much attracting, and distracting our attention. So often we are doing the non-urgent and non-important work. This is a distraction. Or we delude ourselves by doing 'urgent but not important work.' Steve was so tied up doing the 'do' all the time, that he had no time for himself. He could not get into what is called "The Zone." "Important work" is sometimes taking time for ourselves and reflecting on what is important and worthwhile. Steve wasn't taking time to reflect on what he was, or was not doing that was affecting so many people.

Let me ask you, when was the last time you actually sat in a chair with a coffee and did nothing but think for at least 20 minutes? Yes, I know you're smiling, because most of us have never done it. We're too busy!

With technology the way it is, we are constantly connected to some form of social media that inhibits us just having time to sit, relax, think and reflect. We are all busy being busy, and don't take time for ourselves. This is a fundamental flaw in the way we live and operate today. It makes us busy constantly, answering texts, being on Facebook or Instagram or any one of the other myriad of social media platforms. Just by reading this book you have made a change in the way you operate because you have taken time out for yourself to sit and relax, think and reflect.

The power of "Me Time" is important in our day to day functioning as an individual. If you recall it's where I started on my journey – the Outward Bound experience…that's where the epiphany occurred for me.

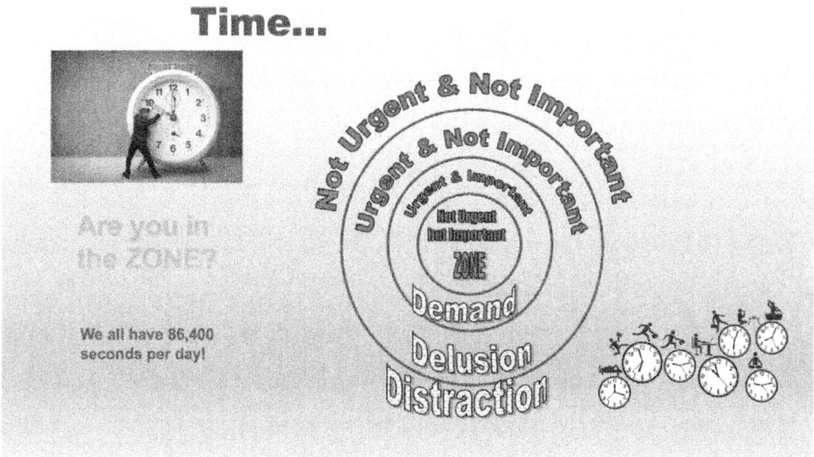

There is always someone to help or to stay in touch with, or answer on a social media platform. Getting time to actually take a deep breath for yourself is part of being 'balanced' – even diet, exercise, and healthy choices are important to you as an individual.

While going away to F1 events and having two week holidays with your friends might be negative if you haven't balanced it with family time, there also has to be a window for individual as well as collective regeneration? Remember it's so important to have a bit of Me time

Habits

Habits either work for or against you. Take any habit you practice and times it by 365 days, then times it by 70 or 80 years and you can write your obituary. If you're serious about changing your life, you must stop practising bad habits and start instituting good ones.

Life is nothing more than the sum total of many successful years...

...a successful year is nothing more than the sum total of many successful months...

...a successful month is nothing more than the sum total of many successful weeks...

...a successful week is nothing more than the sum total of many successful days

That's why practising successful habits, day in and day out, is the most certain way to win over the long term.

A thought

School teaches you about Maths, English and Science. It doesn't teach you about relationships or marriage. You are guided by your parents' relationship (good or bad) or your peers.

Relationships are the most important aspect of your life, yet you go into it with very little training from previous relationships. You may have got those wrong, meaning your marriage is now based on previous mistakes that you thought were right because you don't know any different.

A story about Michael Schumacher

Michael said the following which also applies to relationships;

"If you don't invest the effort, you don't get the performance.

To be at the top, whatever your field, you have to give 100%. The only thing that has changed, the thing I have developed with age and experience, is the **quality**. *I've improved the content of what I do. I'm not just talking as a driver but as a person. Over time, I have understood lots of things I didn't have a clue about before.*

"First and foremost, you have to respect the performance of even the smallest opponent. Meticulousness and discipline are two things, because it is in fact in triumph that you have to look more carefully for your own weaknesses than in defeat.

"Never think that success is down to your own performance alone. If you start in a rush of exuberance, listening only to yourself and controlling everything yourself, you will take the first step back toward the bottom. The flowers of victory belong in many vases.

"Success never comes from one recipe. It's a big combination of many things which have to be together to be successful whatever area of sport or other business you want to be successful in.

"You should never have methods, only principles. Seeking perfection, humility and honesty are things that are important."

Juan Manual Fangio, another great driver, once said; "*You must always believe you will become the best, but you must never believe you have done so.*"

Two of the greatest drivers in the history of F1, and they could just as well be giving the formula for a successful business or marriage. Success can never be put down to one person. There are a lot of people who make up a good relationship or business.

Look at world leaders. They have multitudes of aides to assist them with all the plethora of briefings, memos, decisions and politics they have to deal with on a daily basis. They are unable to do it all by themselves. They must be connected to others to help them, just as we must be connected in our business or relationship.

Dr Thomas Sowell, author and senior fellow at the Hoover Institute, said about government;

"It is hard to imagine a more stupid or more dangerous way of making decisions than by putting those decisions in the hands of people who pay no price for being wrong".

This is true for any business venture or relationship as well.

Managing family and business

I still go back to something I learnt from Lee Iacocca who said;

"If you can't be at home for dinner at 6:00 with your family, you're running your business wrong."

Someone who has a job working 10-12 hour days still struggles with managing time, family and their job. Managing a business and family is not much different than a person who's crazily committed to their work.

For a business owner, it's a bit different because you never stop working. You're working 24 hours a day. However, being the owner means you can set it up to be any way you want.

"You should never have methods, only principles. Seeking perfection, humility and honesty are things that are important."

That means you've got to set your business up so that it works for you, rather than you working for it. It should be the goal of the business owner for your employees to be busy, not for you to be busy.

As a business owner, you've got to add in even more. You've got to add in friends. You've got to add in health. You've got to add in the wealth-building side of your life. You've got to add in the fun and the enjoyment part.

What happens when people go into business for themselves? The business becomes a be-all and end-all; it becomes the central theme of everything.

One of the keys to leadership and relationships is having the hard discussions early. When you sit down with an employee, you don't want to have the hard discussions later; you need them at the front end. When you sit down with a business partner, you want to have the hard discussions up front; "Who's doing what by when? How will we handle the money? Who is responsible for what?"

Family communication

These hard discussions don't seem to happen in personal relationships; the tough times become the tough times because nobody talks about the issues.

It is one of the major issues that you must resolve to have a harmonious relationship and business that work in tandem together. Have those conversations early. The longer you leave it, the harder it becomes. If you abdicate having the discussion, you are abdicating your responsibility.

A story

When I got together with Janelle and I realised the relationship was going somewhere, I told her we needed to sit down and talk. We needed to have an open and honest discussion about what we wanted in the relationship and about our past so nothing can come back to bite us. This is one of the most profound things I have done in my life. We both opened up about our failings, our vulnerabilities, our joys, our achievements, our desires for the future and what we wanted from, and for each other.

Janelle's side of failure and vulnerability lasted all of 20 minutes, whereas, after two and a half days of listening to mine, Janelle asked if it would be alright to stop for a cup of coffee and asked how much longer I still had to go! It was enlightening and invigorating to start a relationship off with such honesty and clarity. We could go into the relationship with our eyes wide open knowing that we had been completely honest and open with each other.

Couples often go to couples therapy or counselling where the counsellor makes them have those hard discussions. And it is probably the first time that they have been held accountable to have those discussions together.

You need to approach the running of the family home as you would a business. Everyone needs to play their part.

Do you have an organisational chart? Do you have job descriptions and roles? Who does what?

If you haven't sat down with your family and decided who does what and who's responsible for doing what things, then do so. Being organised is hard. It's one of the key skills to great leadership, and in a family, you need a leader.

Not everyone can be the leader at all times in the family. For different events, different people need to be the leader. If you haven't decided who's the leader, it's very tough.

Simple things, like rules at the dinner table, can make a huge difference. Have everyone put their phones and iPads away. Tell the children stories. Have a quiz session. Ask them about their day. What was the best thing about the day? What was the most challenging thing about their day?

The kids might hate it to begin with, but soon they will start to enjoy the dinner table. It will be central to the family. Those quick 10-minute dinners where the family wolfed down the food to get back to their computer games, will stop. Dinner will extend into hour-long discussions and real family time.

I often hear people say; "I have quality time with my kids and not quantity time". I have never understood this concept; quite frankly, I believe it is drivel and an abdication of responsibility.

Kids prefer it if you went for a walk with them and chatted with them, rather than going and buying them a new toy.

Employees need your time until they have the processes in place to be able to do it without you. Your children are like employees and want quantity of time with you until they are at the stage where they are leaving home, and your job is done.

In saying that though, is your job ever done with the children? I know for a lot of parents, their kids leave home, struggle and move back again or continue to need support…I'm not sure that a parent's job is ever quite done?

It's not just children. It's your spouse or partner too. **Time is a big indicator of love.**

The biggest part of a relationship is showing up, actually being there when you said you would. Be there for the important things. Do you turn up for work in your business? Why would it be different with your family?

There is a balance to this though. The times our kids and employees live in now are different. And when our kids move into the world of business and have their own family, it will be different for them as well. They will need to learn to adapt, just as we are.

You might get frustrated about them being on their phone. They're Snapchatting or texting with their mates. It's just a different world than the one you and I grew up in. My child might be in the same room as me but be on the phone to their friends. When I was a kid, I wasn't even in the room. I'd be on my bike or walking around the hills playing games with my mates and Mum wouldn't see me until dinner time.

I recall getting told off by a friend's mother for calling round to their place to see if my friend wanted to play. The fact it was 7.15 am on Sunday morning was lost on me. I was up and ready to play. Why on earth was she upset? I wasn't early; I was ready for that day's adventures.

Each generation has a different methodology for raising the current generation. I would rather my kids had a phone problem than a drug problem. The fact that the family is sitting at a table together rather than the kids not even being there is an extraordinary gift to give them.

Wake up

How do we get business owners to wake up to the idea that family matters?

I say to them; "Hey, mate, your relationship is suffering because of your work."

You need to build a commercial, profitable enterprise that works without you.

This entails systemising your operations.

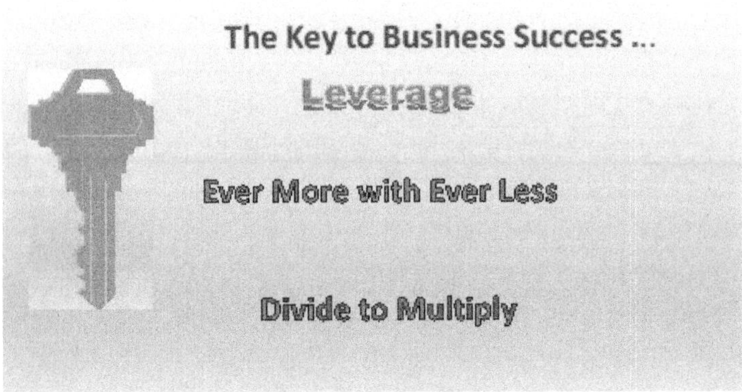

If you have to be at work, it's not a business; it's a job.

Leverage is about 4 key areas in the business:

1. Systems and Technology
2. Delivery and Distribution
3. Testing and Measuring and Accounting
4. People and Education

You Leverage this by putting it into a system.

A system is all about

S aving
Y our
S elf
T ime
E nergy &
M oney.

It's leveraging your time. Remember Pareto's principle – the 80:20 rule.

80% of works gets done in 20% of the time allocated,

or

80% of the work gets done by 20% of the staff.

Therefore in business

SYSTEMISE the ROUTINE, and HUMANISE the EXCEPTION.

Leverage what you can. I so often hear business owners say, "Oh, I'm so busy." This is so silly. You need to have your staff being busy, not you. Leverage your time so you're working strategically on the things that make you money in the business. Let your staff be busy doing the technical or sales stuff.

This will free you up to have time with family or friends, and do the things in life that are important to you.

You've got to want to change though. If you don't want to make the change, you're not going to.

Unfortunately, for a lot of people, they get their human needs met better from work than they do with their family. A lot of business owners want to go to work because; "At work, at least they listen to me. At work, at least they do as I ask!"

"At work, when I show up, they take notice because I'm the boss. I come home, and my teenager says; "Yeah, Dad. Right, Dad. Next thing, Dad".

Sometimes it's a fairly hard thing for a person who is the boss in one place to come home and be the 'take out the rubbish guy'. You need to understand you have different roles in different places in life.

That's just how it is. You go to work where you're the guru, and everyone listens to you, then you come home, and it's; "Hey, can you drive me to football practice?"

You're now the taxi driver. You're not the business guru because your teenager doesn't care. They want to get to football practice and have a great time with their mates. If you're not happy with your role, then change your role, but you can't expect it to be something different than what it is.

A realisation as to why there is so much separation

When I was doing my Outward Bound and was wide awake in my little hide all by myself, I had a huge BFO (Blinding Flash of the Obvious).

I didn't want to be saved.

I don't think many people want to be saved. They want to blame the business or relationship rather than saying; "Hey, I don't want to be here anymore." I realised as I sat there in the dark that this was me.

The reason they don't want to be here is that they've seen more. It's very hard to be in a relationship with someone who you've grown apart from.

If you go to seminars and learn a whole bunch of stuff and your partner doesn't go with you, then you grow apart. If you go on vacations to different places and meet a whole bunch of new people and you've got a whole group of new friends that your partner doesn't have, you grow apart.

I was very much into Property Investing, and it was my enjoyment, my baby. My wife wasn't interested, and I was dragging her along against her will.

I was in the wrong.

It was something I wanted, as opposed to something we wanted. I had a selfish desire. This was just another incident that drove us apart. At the time, I couldn't see it, and I chose not to have the hard conversation to rectify the issue.

You've got to grow together. It's a simple thing. If you don't grow together, it's very difficult for a relationship to stand. You've got to build a group of friends together. You've got to have interests together.

If you don't have a date night every week, then how do you expect the relationship to stay active and healthy? You fell in love by going on dates two or three nights a week. You don't stay in love by not going on any dates.

Do it together. If you're running a business, and your wife is saying; "You're not home enough," say; "Well, great, come and help me out at work then. Come and help me, bring the kids and let's do something together. Let's work on it together".

I had one of my clients years ago who said; "At night, I have to do this because that's going to get sales. I can't be at home."

I said; "Great, get the kids, pick up dinner and do it together at the office."

If your kids have to ask you; "What is it you do?" then you know there's a problem.

Take your family along to your business so they can see it, so they can be a part of it, so they can understand it. Let them get to know the people you work with and all the stuff that happens on a day-to-day basis. Then they can say; "Wow, so that's what you do". Take them along to your workshops and seminars so the kids can see you present.

Bring the kids into the office and have them help out. Do it together. It's easy to think you've got to do it all on your own and not ask for help and not involve them. Making money is not one person's responsibility, it's the family's responsibility. If you worked on a farm, guess what? The kids would be involved. If you ran a restaurant and you all lived above the restaurant, amazingly all the kids would help out.

Give your children a backstage pass to go behind the scenes of your company. Show them how your business works.

What could be more boring than commercial fishing or ice road truckers? Yet, the Discovery Channel made a great success out of documenting these. People are interested in things, so are your children.

Family and business should not be mutually exclusive. The two should be combined. The family should be involved in the business, and the business person should be involved in the family. You've got to combine the two.

A story

I remember Michael asking me if he could come to one of my workshops. I said, "Sure, why not." Here was this 13-year-old sitting amongst all these property investors and they were looking at him. I cued Michael to ask a particular question during the workshop that just floored everyone with its sophistication and skill. I gave a straight-faced answer and asked him if that had answered his question. He thanked me and said it had. The delegation erupted into applause at the question from this 13-year-old.

At that stage, I had to come clean and let the delegates know that Michael was my son and he had asked to come along so he could see and listen to what I did for my work. Three people came up to me after the workshop asking me how I got my children interested in my work. They had not been able to do this in their family.

There's a reason they call it a "family business" and that's because the family gets involved. If only one person in the family is running the business, it's hard for everyone else in the family to understand it.

But your wife or husband may say; "Well, hang on, I've got my own job, and I'm employed somewhere else. I'm doing my eight hours, and then you want me to come into the business and work some more?"

It's a simple answer.

If your partner is having trouble with something and needs help cooking the dinner, then you should dive in and help cook the dinner. You don't sit there and say; "I've done my part for the day. I've done my 12 hours".

If someone is that selfish that they're not going to help, then how are you hoping the future will get better.

Marriage is not 50/50. Marriage is 100 and 100. At some point, your spouse or partner may not be able to put in 100% so you will have to.

Having a relationship is work. Having a relationship with someone else who has different needs, wants and desires to you, is work. If you think a marriage or relationship should be easy, then maybe you should be packing it up and going; "Yep, okay. I really shouldn't have done this relationship thing, because I'm not actually willing to do it".

If that's the case, admit to yourself that you're not willing to do the work, and move on.

If you're willing to do the work, then you'll come home from your 12-hour shift by 6 pm, and you'll go and help out your spouse or partner for a couple of hours with their business because it's your business too. It's not their business; it's both your business. Everything is 'ours' when you're married.

I hate it when I hear; "Dad is babysitting". Rubbish! He's the Dad. He's parenting. I get blown away when people say; "Oh, you're taking care of the kids for the weekend. Have you got someone helping you out?"

"No. I'm the Dad. I'm quite capable of taking care of my children."

I'm talking co-involvement in all aspects of business and family.

Getting the synergy right between you is important. You can have both together, but you have to work hard at it together. Let me repeat that word; together.

If you don't let your family help out, they can't understand what's happening. They can't have empathy, sympathy or compassion for you because they don't even see it.

They don't even know what your business is.

They don't know what your vision is.

Have the hard discussions and make the hard decisions early on. Don't wait. Meet trouble half way and do something about it. Don't wait for it to get right to the end.

Like a snowball, it starts small. If you put it on a hill, it will start rolling down, slowly at first. As it picks up speed, it collects 'debris' along the way, until it becomes a great unwieldy mass that has generated so much power and momentum that it is incapable of stopping. And when it does finally crash, the effect is so profound that it explodes apart, discharging the 'debris', everywhere and others become embroiled in the consequence.

Deal with the snowball while it is still small and manageable.

New rules

The rules of the world have changed. The rules of the family have changed. It's not "the husband's job to make money and the wife's job to stay at home and take care of the kids". The rules of the game have changed. Everyone does everything these days.

Understand what you want

Unfortunately, there will be a lot of people who are trying to get ahead in life but keep getting pulled down by the people around them. This can be especially difficult when those people are your extended family. You must be strong and make sure you spend less time with people who don't encourage you and challenge you to become the best you can be.

Always remember that who you're becoming is far more important than what you're doing. It is what you're doing that is determining who you're becoming. Remember **BE X DO = HAVE**. You are awakening your **BE**. These are the parts of you under the water of the iceberg that nobody else sees as you change.

Mark Hammett, when Head Coach for the Wellington Hurricanes Rugby team, had this to say which reflects well in business, family and sport;

"Your on-field performance is a direct reflection of your off-field performance. If you're inconsistent in your life off-field, you'll be inconsistent on-field.

"We need to give more than we expect back. Is there ever a time you were given something that made you feel better than when you gave something. People always feel better when they give.

"Culture doesn't start with performance on the field. It's about what you're prepared to do for the team. Culture begins in little things like how you treat your teammates. If you do the right thing, then you start growing relationships, then you care about each other. That creates culture. Get that right, and intrinsic things like a harder edge, poise under pressure and defensive fortitude start kicking in.

"It's about standards. If you take shortcuts outside the game/work, you'll take shortcuts inside the game/work. Then when you have to take the long way round, you don't know where that is.

"The behaviours you walk past are the behaviours you accept."

These thoughts are so applicable to family and business. Every family, just like business, has its own culture. Each person, individually or collectively, decided whether that culture is toxic or healthy. If it's healthy, the family or business unit thrives.

John Anderson says that business and family is about negotiation. To negotiate, put yourself in the other person's shoes. It's not just what you want but also what the other person wants. If you can satisfy within reason what the other person wants, you'll more often get what you want in return.

Successful businesses and family revolve around people, their relationships and mutual trust and cooperation. There is no substitute for quality.

What do your customers/spouse/partner want? Don't write answers down. **Listen.**

The requests that matter will be the ones you hear over and over again. It will become as loud as a beating drum when you start listening.

Many people in business won't 'give' a little. They believe they must win at all costs, regardless of the other person in the relationship. Rarely does this strategy work.

Your relationship and business are like a Report Card. We all read the same words but interpret what is said differently. We interpret what we read to build a mental picture, but it may be a different mental picture to our partner, whether business or personal. Not until we fully immerse ourselves into the relationship do we all sing off the same page in the hymnbook.

Strong opinions aren't free. You'll turn some people off. You'll be accused of being arrogant and aloof. That's just life. For everyone who loves you, there will be others who hate you. If nobody is upset by what you're saying, you're probably not pushing hard enough. When you don't know what you believe, everything becomes an argument. But when you stand for something, decisions are obvious.

my learnings:

- ☑ Your business should work for you rather than you working for your business
- ☑ Have the hard discussions early
- ☑ My family relationships are as important as my business relationships, so I must work on them just as hard

Your learnings:

- [ ]
- [ ]
- [ ]

I hate tea!

I was the 'first mate' on the boat. Dad had bestowed this title upon me as a six-year-old, and I felt so proud. OK, so our boat was only 16ft long, and my Dad was the skipper. Being the first mate though, wow, what an honour.

Dad used to be Head Surgeon for P&O shipping lines, so he had grown up around water and boats. He only left the sea because he met my Mum and the ship's officers weren't allowed wives on board. So, Mum and Dad jumped off the boat in Perth for three years, before sailing across the Tasman and settling in New Zealand.

Dad and I would go fishing together on Lake Taupo in New Zealand. We would anchor the boat in the mouth of the Tongariro River as it gushed its contents into the world-famous Lake Taupo. We would be there fishing from just before sunrise until about 11.30 am.

As the 'first mate', it was my job to make the tea. Dad, being Irish, liked his tea; and I mean, he *really* liked his tea. About every 15th fly cast, I had to stop fishing and go and make tea from one of the big thermoses.

Out of six hours of potential fishing time, I probably only managed about 40 minutes. The rest of the time I was making tea.

No matter what I said or tried or did to persuade Dad that I was sick of making the tea, it forever fell to me, the first mate, to make it.

I realised then that I was never going to join the Navy and I was never going to be a tea-drinker.

A huge BFO came to me from this about relationships and working together. I realised Dad was teaching me a very valuable lesson. Jobs need to be done, and even the most menial task needs someone to do it. So do it cheerfully.

Doing the menial tasks makes you appreciate the good tasks when they come along. Even now, when I am doing something I don't enjoy, I think back to being the 'first mate' and making the tea. I realise whatever I am doing now, pales in comparison to my constant tea-making days. It **takes courage** to continue doing those menial tasks and making a difference.

Courage is displayed at unexpected moments, and what I do in such moments can change me, and those around me.

A story I often refer to is of a spy who was sentenced to death by a Persian General.

The General had a strange tradition of giving condemned criminals the choice of a firing squad or the 'big door'.

When the General asked which will it be, the spy chose the firing squad. Turning to his aide, the General said; "They always prefer the known to the unknown, yet we give them a choice."

The aide asked; "What is beyond the big door?"

The General replied; "Freedom," then he added, "Few are brave enough to take that door".

The dividing line between mediocrity and success is courage. That's why David told his son Solomon upon ascending to the throne; "***Be strong and of good courage, and do it***".

Don't give up:

I love this poem that I found somewhere about 30 years ago. I have no idea who the author is, but I reproduce it to honour such wonderful thoughts and words

'When things go wrong as they sometimes will, and the road you're trudging seems all uphill.

When funds are low, and the debts are high, and you want to smile, but you have to sigh.

When things are pressing you down a bit, rest if you must, but don't you quit!

Life is strange with its twists and turns, as every one of us sometimes learns,

And many a failure turns about when he might have won if he'd stuck it out.

Don't give up, though the pace seems slow - you might succeed with another blow.

Often the goal is nearer than it seems, to a faint and faltering man.

Often the struggler has given up, when he might have captured the victor's cup.

And he learned too late, when the night slipped down, how close he was to the golden crown.

Success is failure turned inside out - the silver tint of the clouds of doubt.

You never can tell how close you are, it may be near when it seems afar.

So stick to the fight when you're hardest hit - it's when things seem worst that you mustn't quit.'

The Taps in Life

There are problems in the world every day. These problems go around and around. If they are not fixed, they just get bigger and bigger.

I call these the taps on the motorway of life.

They are similar to the rumble strips on the road. As we drift close to the roadside, we hit the rumble strip. It makes an almighty Brrrrrrrrrrrrrr noise. It lets you know you're getting too close to the roadside, and you need to do something about it.

Do you do something about it or not?

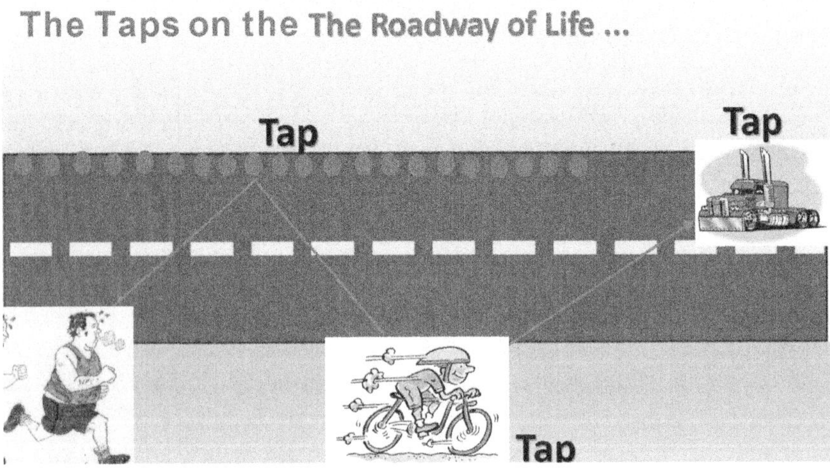

Taps start small. We have an issue that needs resolving, but we do nothing about it. That is like a tap on the shoulder, the rumble strip on the road. It doesn't hurt too much but it does remind us that there is something we need to take care of.

In health; a niggling pain that comes and goes.
In relationships; you start to have more fights.
In business; your cash flow isn't there.

We shrug it off. We hope it will go away.

Next, we get a tap on the back of our head. The problem has got bigger; you've nearly driven into the barrier arm. The issue rises again, like a fountain of steam. Again, we do nothing, hoping it will just go away, so we don't have to deal with it.

Another tap. This one is more like riding a bike and falling off. This one hurts, we get bruised and cut skin with a bit of blood flowing but still doesn't hurt enough for us to take action.

Finally, having taken no notice of the previous taps, you drive off the road or into the face of an oncoming truck.

This is serious.

This tap has consequences.

You've got to take notice of those taps on the shoulder and start to say;

-"Hey, I'm not quite in the place where I want to be in my relationship".

"Hey, I'm not quite in the place where I want to be in my business".

"Hey, I haven't quite got the cash flow I need in my business to pay those bills right now".

Everything in life is just a decision. If only we'd sorted out the lack of cash flow three months earlier when we got the first tap.

If only you had listened to your spouse or partner when they let you know they were frustrated at you working too many hours and not spending time with the family.

Now the issue is so large you have to do something about it; you have a crisis that needs resolving.

"Why didn't I heed the first tap when I could have done something about it easily?"

It could be that you don't have enough money because you're doing sales wrong or you don't have enough cash flow because you're doing your accounting wrong.

It might not be one segment of business you are doing wrong; it could be multiple segments of business. It's just a lack of knowledge on the business owner's behalf. We don't go into business knowing everything we need to know about how to run a business.

You might be a good chef, so you open a restaurant. Or you might be a good accountant, so you open an accounting business.

That doesn't mean you know how to recruit, hire, and train people. It doesn't mean you know how to make sales or how to be a manager or how to do marketing. All of these things you have to learn as a business owner. The hardest work for a business owner is the learning work, not the doing work. The doing work is relatively easy because you probably had a job where you were doing it before.

Invariably, in business and our relationships, we let issues slide or don't deal with the problem that is right in front of us. We are scared of hurting the other person, or we don't know how to resolve the issue effectively; we think that by doing nothing, it may go away.

In life, this doesn't happen. It's like a snowball rolling down the hill, it gets bigger and bigger and rolls faster and faster until the momentum is such that it takes on a life of its own.

It's abdicating our responsibility.

When Apollo 13 ran into trouble en-route to the Moon, Gene Krantz, the Flight Director uttered the immortal words – "**Failure is not an option.**" The team went to work to solve the issue and bring the Astronauts back to earth - alive. This was their business. Nothing else mattered. Getting to the moon was now not the object; getting the astronauts home was.

We have always gazed at the moon from our earthly home. Our wonder at the beauty and majesty of the moon has been perpetual since time began and humans looked up at it.

An old Kabati adage from Korea says; **We must strive to be like the moon**

People complain when there is too much sun and it gets unbearably hot, and also when it rains too much or when it is too cold. But no-one grumbles when the moon shines. Everyone becomes happy and appreciates the moon in their own special way. Children watch their shadows and play in its light. People gather in squares to tell stories and tramp through bush and mountainous terrain at night by its light. A lot of happy things happen when the moon shines. These are some of the reasons you should want to be like the moon.

- Grow tolerant
- Reflect on the past, plan for the future
- Learn the virtues of love, modesty and making concessions
- Become broad-minded with strong faith
- Have the right mindset
- Understand how nature works, not grow greedy

- Think in a healthy manner, and do the right things
- Grow trusting and patient
- Have strong relationships
- Learn creativity and wisdom
- Learn how to live reasonably and form mutual understanding in the community.
- Feel that we are part of mother nature.

The Cycle of Business

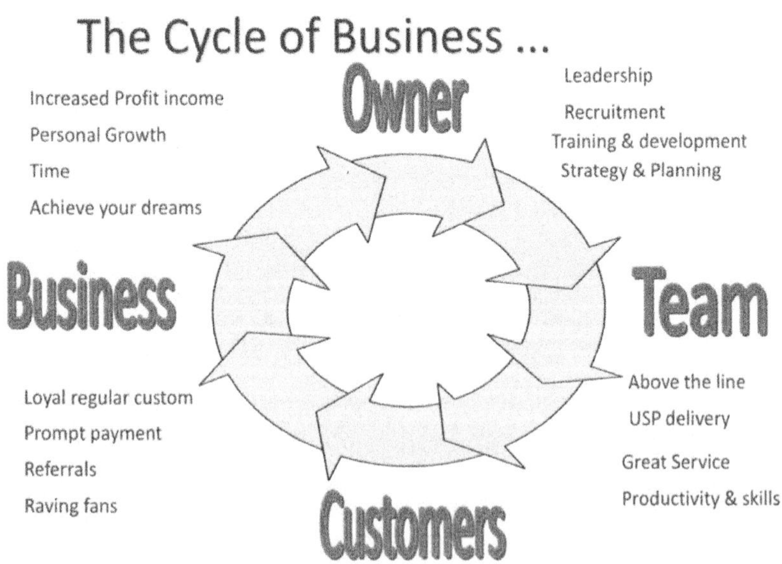

Many Business Owners believe that to be a successful business owner, they must run the Team, look after the Customers, and run all aspects of the Business. **STOP**, this is plain wrong. There is a cycle to being a Business Owner and it goes like this.

You as a Business Owner must look atter the team.

You do this by providing:

- Great leadership
- Having good recruitment strategies
- Having great training and development systems
- Having transparent Strategies to grow the business.

The TEAM are required to:

- Always play "Above the Line of Success"
- Deliver great customer service
- Use their skills in the best possible way to grow the business
- Upselling and cross-selling where appropriate
- Listening to customers needs and wants and fulfilling those

The CUSTOMERS help the Business by:

- Promptly paying all invoices within the correct timeframe
- Becoming raving fans of the business
- Referring their friends and family to the business
- Regularly doing business with you.

The BUSINESS help you by:

- Giving you time away from the business for family and friends
- Providing the cash to achieve your dreams and have those family holidays
- Growing you as a person

High Performance Teams:

One of the most important aspects that any business needs, to get to the top and to remain there, is to develop a High Performing Team. The key to an HPT is engagement. This is the 'sweet-spot' in the middle of the 3 circles.

Ensuring your Team are engaged is one of the most important keys any Business Owner needs to understand. A worldwide study by Gallup (2017) found that on average 87% of the worldwide workforce was disengaged or highly disengaged. It is costing Business Owners 34% of the salary they pay out to employees. Imagine for every $10,000 you pay out, $3,400 is wasted and unproductive.

What this means is if your business were a ship, then 2 of your employees are engaged, 6 or 7 are doing just what is required, and will leave if they get a better job with more pay, and only 1 or 2 are doing more than is expected.

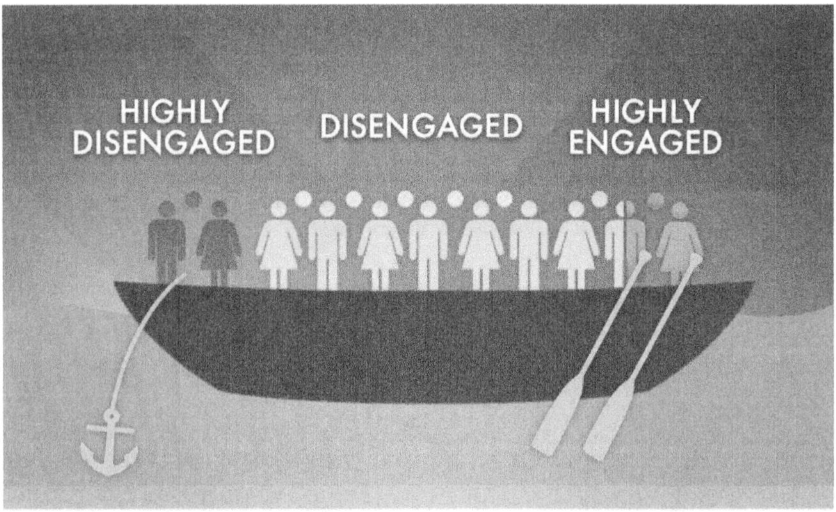

Former US Secretary of State, Colin Powell, made a powerful observation when addressing the 2009 Global Leaders Lecture series;

"Everyone in a team knows who is and who is not performing, and they are looking to you as the leader to see what you are going to do about it."

The 3 pillars to ensuring a functioning HPT are *Culture, Leadership* and *Skillset*. Notice that 2 pillars without the 3rd only give us one benefit. All three must be achieved together.

For example, *Leadership* and *Culture* together, without *Skillset*, only gives you the benefit of Loyalty. Productivity and Excellence are left out of the equation. Both are important to achieve an HPT. *Skillset* and *Leadership* without *Culture* only gives us the benefit of Excellence.

You need all 3 pillars in conjunction with each other and intertwined to give the 3 benefits of Loyalty, Productivity and Excellence. This leads to engagement across the whole spectrum of business. From these 3 pillars are 9 sub-pillars. 3 for each main pillar. These nine sub-pillars play an integral part in achieving the Engaged 'sweet spot' within a team.

When a team focuses on these 9 keys they start maximising the returns they obtain by ensuring they understand and develop the process for achieving great results. The business grows as a result. This in turn leads to a very happy and engaged workforce which means productivity increases, solutions are looked for, and found by staff.

Let's pick *Culture* and look at the 3 sub-pillars. Let's look at "*Solution Focus*" first. Many business owners have what I call an 'open door policy.' This is one of the worst management philosophies you can adopt. What you're saying to your staff is, come in an interrupt me at any time. Don't think for yourself.

Have an open door policy by all means, but only for a certain time or times during the day. For example, say between 10 – 11am and again between 2.30 – 3.30pm. And when staff come to see you with a problem, they <u>must</u> bring a solution for the problem as well. It may not be the correct solution, or one you want to implement but what it does is start staff thinking for themselves. After a while they will form the habit of *solution focussed* thinking when they come to see you. It will free up more of your time. It means also that they will probably resolve the problem, before they see you because they can't be bothered to wait for your answer. A win for everyone!

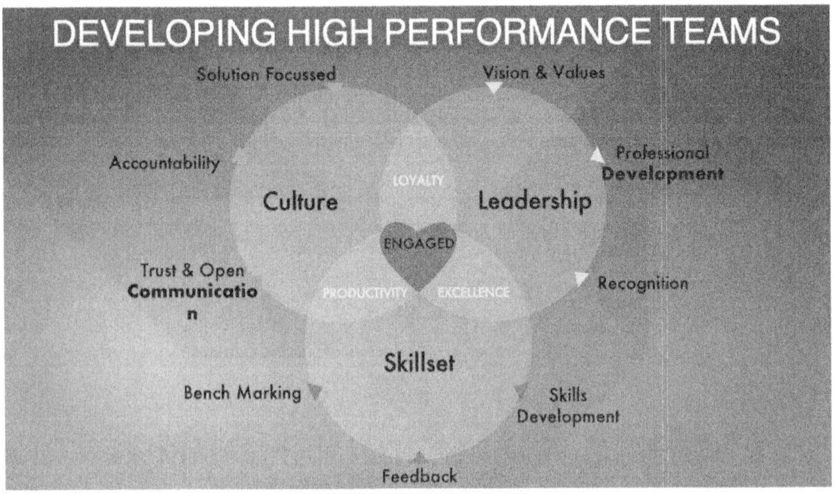

The next benefit and sub-pillar is *Accountability.* This is so important in any business. When people understand the KPI's (Key Performance Indicators) that they are responsible for, and being measured against, then behaviour and performance is easy to measure. Always ensure *Accountability* is a key to running your business. When everyone becomes accountable it ensures the business maintains the upward transition

The last sub-pillar is *Trust* and *Open Communication.* When you have this pillar, staff feel empowered. They won't lie. Staff only lie for 2 reasons:

1. They are protecting something or someone.
2. They are scared of an outcome

Building trust is so important and is very fragile. It is not easily won and can be lost so easily.

Trust is about being congruent. Congruent in your actions, your communication and how you conduct yourself. Your staff are watching you. Your integrity and honesty let them know what you will accept and won't accept. Your communication with them and they way you communicate let them know what you will accept and won't accept. Remember the adage, Praise in public, remonstrate behind closed doors. You staff will thank you for it.

These sub-pillars present opportunities to the leadership team, who ensure reward and recognition takes place and great feedback is given and received. Leaders are now leading and the Vision and Values of the organisation are adhered to. Benchmarking becomes the norm, and Skill Development is sought and asked for. Loyalty and a culture of Excellence develops with each individual not wanting to let the team down. Sick days reduce, absences reduce and productivity increase to levels not seen in the organisation. The Heart of the organisation – engagement flows throughout.

As the owner of a high-performance business, you need to:

- Perform to your best in all situations and under any circumstances, coping with the pressures of business ownership, both physically and mentally
- Lead by example and inspire others
- Manage a balance between life and work and have enough energy to enjoy both to the maximum
- Be effective at developing and maintaining a high level of self-management, stress-management and people-management
- Be effective at creating goals and successful management strategies that will impact on the business, people and the bottom line
- Interact with your team in a positive, proactive way that will enable business opportunities and personal opportunities to be maximised
- Personally maintain, and encourage your team to maintain a good degree of fitness and health that will enhance personal welfare and business productivity and efficiency

(If you want to know more about HPT's then contact me – details at the end of this book)

Richard Moloney in his book, 'The Minds of Winning Teams', says that he doesn't think a lot of people have done the study on how to start a business. "It's tough work. Not many people have researched it. They're going to go through the graveyard of hell for three years to get out the other end."

We live in a world where competition is ten times fiercer than it was five years ago because of the internet. Everything's faster. You're not starting a business; you're just employing yourself.

Stress levels are personified ten times because you're putting so much on the line.

7 keys to a winning team

In business and your relationship, certain elements must happen to be successful. There are **7 keys to a winning team**

I learnt this lesson early on in my business career but didn't take it into the matrimonial home which had devastating consequences, the breakdown of my marriage, as you have already read.

There were only 6 keys, but I have added the 7th key. This came about as a great friend and mentor of mine, James Vincent, described it to me.

The 7 keys are as fundamental in a family as they are in business.

7 Keys to A Winning Team ...

1. Strong Leadership
2. Common Goal
3. Rules of the Game
4. Action Plan
5. Support Risk Taking
6. 100% Involvement/Inclusion
7. Ongoing Training & development

1. Strong leadership

Imagine a place without a leader, an army without a General. Structure creates order, without it no progress can be made.

You should respect those in authority above you and honour those who have lived longer than you because they possess a wealth of knowledge. Until you learn to take orders, you will never be qualified to give them. If you rebel against instruction, you can't complain if those around you rebel against your words or opinions.

2. Common Goals

You have goals in your business. What are the goals for your family or your marriage? What is the achievement to be reached?

3. Rules of The Game

Every business and every family has its own set of unique rules to play by. Everyone needs to adhere to these rules; otherwise, there is chaos.

Children need rules or parameters. Children gain great comfort by having parameters that they can bounce off. They know the boundaries.

A story on rules of the game: The goal posts

Sport played such an integral part of Michael's life. He was forever breaking something or losing a ball as a result of some mighty kick into the bushes, the ball being hurled over neighbours' fences or smashing through a window.

He would often be late home from some sporting event or another. His mother and I were beside ourselves trying to come up with some way to let him know he was pushing the boundaries too far.

Each new incident and subsequent punishment led us to believe we'd cracked it, only for Michael to have that bewildered look on his face, wondering what he'd done wrong - again.

To him, it was just sport. The ball may be lost, but he'd find another one. It might have been late and dark when he came home caked in mud, but the game was so much fun he had just lost track of time. And there was always one more goal to score or try to be scored.

One day he asked me to explain the rules of rugby to him. He played football but his brother played rugby, and he wanted to understand what his brother was doing on the field. As I was a rugby referee at the time, he thought I might know a little bit about the laws of the game.

I was explaining the rules to him and had drawn a picture of two goal posts, one at each end of the paper. I was using a magnet to give him a visual reference of when the ball was in play, out of play and where the resulting scrum or line-out would be. He understood this completely. All of a sudden it dawned on me, a Blinding Flash of the Obvious. Here was our way of helping him to understand where on the 'naughty' chart he was.

So, a rugby field was drawn up on a blank piece of paper with the halfway line, goal line, 10m lines, 22m lines and the goal posts. This was placed on the fridge with a rugby ball magnet that I had used when I was explaining the laws of rugby.

We explained to him, anytime the magnet is anywhere between the halfway and 22m lines, you're great, you are doing everything fine. Between 22m lines and goal lines, something is not quite right, and you're pushing the boundaries a little. There could be trouble. When the magnet is between the goal line and dead ball line, you're in big trouble.

If the ball was sailing over the goalposts, Michael was heading for the hills because he knew he was in serious trouble for some major infraction he had committed.

Throughout the day, Michael would come to the fridge and look at where the rugby ball magnet was. When it was out of the halfway and 22m quadrant, he would come and ask what he was doing wrong and what he needed to do to amend his ways. It was such a visual reference for him.

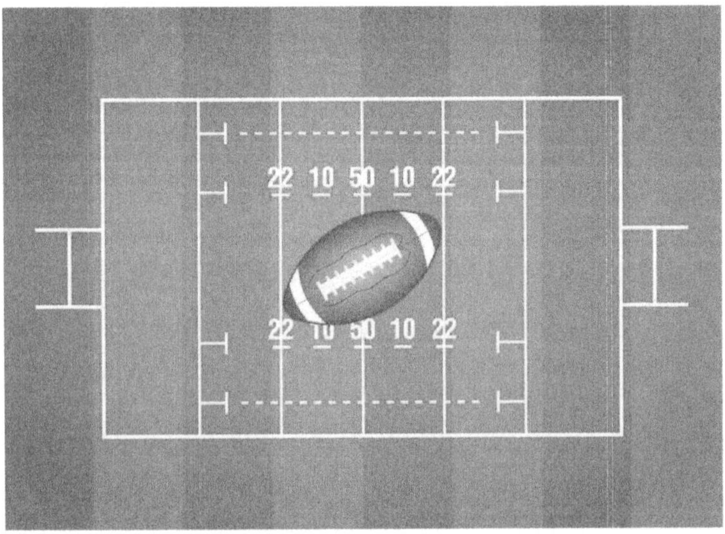

His brother and sister would sometimes come in and shift the magnet into the 'naughty' quadrant. Michael would wonder what on earth he had done wrong. The look of sheer horror on his face was a sight to behold. His brother or sister, still laughing would then return the magnet to its rightful place before his mother or I saw.

Often though, his brother and sister would look after him, and if his Mum or I had put the magnet into the 'naughty' zone, they would shift it back to the halfway line and stand together with Michael with a look of complete innocence on their faces and let us know that was where it had been all along. They had an unwritten rule of looking after each other.

Tip: You can use this model for your own children in their chosen field of sport. If they play hockey, use a hockey field. If they are into athletics, use an athletic track.

4. Action Plan

What is the plan by which we achieve our goals? It's not your business plan; that's for the bank manager when you want a loan.

An action plan is a one-page sheet on which you write actions to be completed in the next 90 days. It is taken from your five-year or one-year vision.

At the end of the book, I have given you three worksheets to help you plan.

The first is your **12-month personal and business goals**. This is your **Vision**.

Ask yourself, three questions to achieving each goal:

1. Why is it important?
2. What do I have to **DO** to get there?
3. What do I have to **BE** to get there?

This again is the **Be x Do = Have** (Results), and shows the importance of this formula.

It is important to do your personal goals first. Out of these will come the business goals needed to achieve your personal goals. Many people do it the other way around. This is not correct. Your business is the conduit to give you a happy personal life.

The second is the **90-day planning sheet** to set actions that will help you achieve the personal and business goals you have set. The 90-day plan is a series of steps taken each week to move you toward your ultimate destination. Breaking down the one-year plan into a 90-day series of steps gives you clarity on the steps needed to get to your goal every week.

Why 90 days? The mind can't work in longer stretches than 90 days, so if you have a 12-month plan, break it into 4 x 90-day plans or steps.

Ensure you take into account things like 'Events' and 'Study' that could inhibit that week's progress. For example, if you have a two-week holiday planned, put it in. If you need to do some study or research before taking an action, put that in. Your time each week should be organised as you set out to achieve your goal.

Progress: What will it feel like at the end of the year if every week you have taken one small step to achieve your ultimate goal? That is

48 steps (allowing for four weeks holiday a year). What will an extra 48 steps look like on your progress scale?

Include your partner and children in the planning and goal setting that you are doing. If they are involved it is more likely they will help you achieve what you desire because they now have a stake in the outcome. They have a vested interest in seeing you succeed because they will receive the reward as well.

5. Support Risk-Taking

Too often, we wrap our kids in cotton wool, hoping that this will keep them away from harm and danger. The problem with this is they have no fear of harm because they don't understand it. They have never felt it. They haven't experienced it. They haven't been allowed to fall out of a tree and hurt themselves. We need to let our kids understand why risk-taking is important and the consequences (and pain) when they get it wrong.

As parents, and with our business, we must support risk-taking.

We still need to mitigate the risks, but employees and children need to take risks to understand boundaries and consequences.

John Anderson in his superb book, 'Just two Seats left,' says; "*Taking risks only seems foolish in retrospect when it doesn't work. When risks do pay off, they are viewed as a stroke of genius. Either way, risk-taking is a necessary part of business*".

To succeed in life both personally and in business, you must take risks. In other words, 'give it a go'. However, mitigate as much of the risk as possible.

The importance of timing and risk-taking

- See what the majority of people are thinking and then consider the opposite as to where the truth may be found
- The crowd is always **late** because they want to be **safe**
- Look online or what's in the Sunday papers or business publications
- Consider each deal, its cash flow position and its potential up-side, on its own merits

6. 100% involvement or inclusion

The only failure is the failure to participate. Parents must have 100% inclusion in their children's lives. In relationships, we must be 100% committed to each other or it won't work.

Business owners must be committed to their employees and include them in the business vision, so they understand what the business owner is striving to achieve. Conversely, employees need to be 100% committed to their boss to ensure the vision happens. The boss provides a livelihood for them. This is why the 12-session Engage and Grow programme is so successful and so fundamental to business growth.

The Engage and Grow model has 37 different keys to success. I have included 12 of them at the end of the book to give you a taste of how it works.

There are six core human needs for inclusion/involvement:

- Love
- Variety
- Growth
- Certainty
- Significance
- Contribution

Love - do you love your employees? Do they love you in return? Is it the same in your marriage?

Variety - is there variety in your work and your relationship?

Growth - are you growing each day to be better?

Certainty - do you have certainty?

Significance - have you got significance in your relationship and your work? Significance for yourself and your family and employees is paramount. Are you and they making the contribution you want?

Contribution - what is the contribution you are making in both areas? Could you be more invested?

The Extra One:

7. Ongoing Training

Number seven in the keys to a winning team. Train, train, train and then train some more. Give everyone the ability to achieve way beyond their expectations.

So often, a team is removed from the office to attend a two-day training course. They come back all excited about their new knowledge. Then, within a week of being back in the same environment, they are reduced to frustration. Their work colleagues who haven't been on the training, continue in the same old ways, reject anything new, and bring the 'converts' down.

This kind of training is one of the reasons why employees are so disengaged today. It's like taking a clean fish out of a dirty pond, putting it in a clean pond, cleaning it and then putting it back in the dirty pond. What do you think happens after one week? The pond is still dirty, and the clean fish is now dirty again and all his excitement and hopes are crushed.

You need to clean the pond and the fishes together.

If you train as a team or family, change the environment. Clean up the environment and family or business together, so everyone is 'clean.'

Don't do the normal training. Use the "Engage and Grow" principle of training.

No business or personal relationship, no matter how ingenious, has the chance of success or will survive, if it is born in the minds of one and carried in the hearts of none.

My learnings:

- [x] The taps in life remind me of where I am failing
- [x] Never give up, no matter how hard the struggle
- [x] Always display courage and make the right choices

Your learnings:

- [ ]
- [ ]
- [ ]

you wanna check out this new game? you try to acquire riches and battle evil forces as you advance through a strange and mysterious world.
sounds awesome, Dad!
© JimBenton.com

Mutual vision

Richard Maloney says; "*Love is about freedom. True love is true freedom, and that true freedom is, 'Babe, I'm going to start a business. I need your full support.' That's freedom to create. That's the only reason why we're here is to experience love and to express ourselves.*"

If I've got a partner who allows me the freedom to do that, with an understanding that there's going to be major potholes on the road to success, then it's hard to say whether it's 50/50 or whether it's give and take. The fact is, it's about having mutual respect. It's actually about 100/100. Both partners giving.

You need to have a mutual vision. You can both create it, but one of you has got to be the leader. When times are tough, someone's got to continually reinforce the vision. Sometimes people mentally spiral down, but one of the partners has got to continually paint the positive picture. Not only do you have to paint it, but you've also got to feel it. You've got to know it, and you've got to believe it, and you've got to own it. You've got to be energetic and clear with where you're going.

Visualising is so important through tough times; in business, as well as your relationship. You've got to show the employees the vision. You've got to get them to buy into the vision. It's the same thing with your partner. Your vision has got to be compelling.

I asked two of my very good friends about their relationships and business. Here is what they had to say:

"Pete, I can speak from experience and past errors. I put a lot of time into starting and running a business when I first arrived in

Blenheim. On selling that business, I then got tied up in a job I loved but spent too much time doing at the expense of my family, and they suffered accordingly. Family should always come first, no matter what. They are the most important part of your life so if you find the right balance, you're doing better than I managed. Ironically my life balance is now almost perfect, and thankfully my family are all happy." **John Alexander**

"It's never easy to balance, is it? I personally found that when life provided some family health challenges that demanded my attention and time, it wasn't as difficult to create space as I thought it was when everything was rosy. After that event had passed, it was actually easy to manage a good balance with the skills I had developed through necessity. My advice would be to imagine you had NO choice and that the time you want with family is non-negotiable. Plan your diary and manage appointments and requirements with that mindset and suddenly it just happens. I wish it hadn't taken a horrible event to make me recognise that but I'm also grateful for the learning." **Tim Rylatt**

Wow, awesome honesty and reality. Thanks guys.

My learnings:

- [x] I must have a vision for my family and business
- [x] My vision must be mutually shared; if it's not, nobody will buy into it
- [x] A relationship should be 100/100

Your learnings:

- [ ]
- [ ]
- [ ]

#2 Engine - Parenting Techniques and Business

Four Trent 900 Rolls Royce engines power the A380 through the sky, giving outstanding fuel economy per passenger mile. Each engine sucks in 1.25 tons of air per second. That's the equivalent of emptying four squash courts of air per second. This air is then mixed with fuel, to make an explosion, that is forcefully pushed out the back, to power the aircraft forward. The pilots have instruments in the cockpit to monitor the performance of each engine and ensure they are obtaining the best performance possible.

In business, what you measure gets done. Testing and measuring is one of the fundamental keys to getting the right efficiencies and effectiveness in your business, just like these giant engines that power the A380. Where the A380 measures fuel economy, in business we need to measure our Gross and Net profit. As the saying goes:

Turnover is vanity

Profit is sanity

Cash is reality

Boundaries

Between my wife and I, we have six children. Raising them meant a very busy and hectic schedule.

What I found interesting was that apparently, we didn't know anything about the world, how to be a good parent or any stuff that was important to make the world function, until our children were around 20. Then, overnight, we were suddenly parents imbued with knowledge and wisdom whom our children would come to seek advice from.

To this day, I am still dumbfounded at our transformation from having no knowledge or wisdom to becoming intellectual giants overnight. We were suddenly the 'fountain of all knowledge" who could now help our children.

Parenting is one of the few 'businesses' in the world, where you are given the test first and then the lesson afterwards. Nothing prepares you for being a parent. School certainly doesn't, and it is one of the hardest roles in life you will ever undertake.

Get it right, and you can raise some delightful, very well-adjusted children who extoll your virtues, values and culture. They will make you proud as they make their way through the world. They will add value to the world they live in and be wonderful members of society. Whatever business they get into, they will excel because you have given them that good start in life by being a good parent and giving them boundaries and parameters to work between.

Get it wrong, and you might end up with wild children who are into drugs and criminal activity, who don't respect authority.

Children who are allowed to push through the boundaries with no consequences end up confused and angry. All they want is to have an understanding of how far they can push and where the 'stop line' is. They want to feel safe and protected. If they take that through to adulthood and break society's boundaries, they can end up being incarcerated, angry and confused. All because nobody gave them parameters to work between in the first instance. They have been let down.

Children need and want boundaries that they can butt up against, so they know and understand limits. This gives children comfort, confidence and a safety net because they learn what is acceptable and what isn't. This allows them to become good members of society. They will thank you for the boundaries you install for them.

A family I know set no boundaries for their son at all; he did what he pleased. Michael tried to befriend him, but unfortunately, they had different values.

Michael invited him to stay over one night, and at the dinner table, this boy did not know how to eat with a knife and fork. Bearing in mind he was aged 11, we found this highly irregular. All he wanted to eat was burgers and chips with his hands. His table manners were appalling.

When it was time for bed, this boy refused, saying he was allowed to stay up late and watch movies. In our house, this didn't wash, so we had 'meaningful dialogue' with him. His eyes became as wide as saucers because nobody had ever sat him down and had a firm chat with him as we did. All of a sudden, he didn't like us and wanted to go home.

When he finally did go to bed, he went to bed fully clothed. We asked him where his pyjamas were. He said he always slept in his clothes because it was easier to get up in the morning. This child had no boundaries whatsoever, and the friendship with Michael was very short-lived. Suffice to say this boy ended up in court several years later on some pretty serious charges.

Parenting

As a parent you don't learn how to be a parent in school or college, you learn it 'on the job'. And you make lots of mistakes; some you may look back on and cringe at. But through it all, you love your children and only want what's best for them.

If your parents failed you, then you probably have wounds that need to be healed. But don't fall into the trap of self-pity by buying into the idea that you came from a 'dysfunctional family'. Some families are better than others, but all of them have areas of dysfunction.

Look back and consider your parents' circumstances and some of the challenges they faced while raising you, and perhaps you'll be able to view the mistakes they made with a little more compassion.

They are human beings, just as you are; they make mistakes, just as you do. Nobody's perfect. By showing compassion towards them, you'll be better able to show compassion towards yourself when you inevitably make the mistakes with your own children.

And - this is important - when your children see you extending grace towards your parents, they'll be better able to extend it towards you.

If you need to forgive your parents, do it today and move on.

The phone technique for daughters

Being a father to a daughter and step-daughter always filled me with dread. They were growing into beautiful, intelligent young women who had the capacity and mental aptitude to do anything. I was determined to ensure they were given every opportunity to make good decisions, even when they felt pressured to do otherwise.

I did not want them pressured by some young 'stud' wanting to place notches on his belt at the expense of my daughters.

Recalling experiences from my younger days made me realise I didn't want any boyfriend of my daughter's trying to emulate my erstwhile ways.

On reflection, I am not proud of what I did in my youth. However, it did give me an insight as to how I could protect my daughters and allow them to control any potentially uncomfortable situation that they may find themselves in.

I took Claire and Louisa aside individually, just before they started dating, and sat them down for probably the most profound father-daughter talk we would ever have.

I said to them; "At some stage in your dating career, you may find yourself in an uncomfortable situation. You may be asked to do something, either sexually or morally, that is wrong or that you feel uncomfortable doing or that you don't want to be a part of."

I went on; "This is what I want you to do. I want you to take out your mobile phone and hand it to the person who is making you feel uncomfortable. Say to them, 'Please ring my Dad. Let him know what you are proposing. If it's OK with him, then it will be OK with me'".

I have not had such a phone call to date. I can only assume 2 situations:

1. That they have never been put in that situation.
2. Alternatively, they are so wild that they have gone along with any, and every wild thing their boyfriends have proposed!

Both daughters have said to me that knowing this allowed them to feel in control. Regardless of the circumstances, they knew they could ring their Mum or me, and we would help them out of the situation that they were finding too difficult to handle. And with no judgement from us whatsoever.

It removes the pressure because they don't have to make the decision. It is placed on me, as the father, and I am happy to have that pressure, so they don't.

It is hard enough being a young woman in this world without the added pressure of being forced to do something you don't want to do.

Business can be like our daughters. You can get into a situation that is beyond your control or understanding, especially when you're new to business.

I still needed a mentor and guide when I was ten years into business because there was so much I didn't know or understand.

I still have a mentor and guide now, some 21 years later, because I know I need it. Someone I can call or talk with, who can guide me and help me understand what the right thing to do is. Someone who doesn't judge me.

It is important to have someone who doesn't judge you or tell others about your mistakes or situation. Someone who can take the pressure from you, so you learn.

Don't be scared to be like my daughters. Have someone in your corner, in your business life that you can call or talk with, who will help with those uncomfortable times.

Dining room table

Manners are important at the dining room table. Mum taught me manners and her expectations. Some things I took on board, others were just too far out of whack for me.

My Aunt Marama was also into good table manners but I felt went a little too far. Most people, if they require the salt or pepper or some other accoutrement, will ask for it to be passed. Not Aunt Marama. She would wait until someone noticed her waiting.

I cottoned onto this pretty fast, as did my good friend Dave Goodwin. Being young and obnoxious, we made a game of it and we pretended we didn't notice her waiting. We would merrily eat away, looking everywhere except in Aunt Marama's direction. We would wait to see how long before someone else noticed, and feign surprise when someone did notice and mentioned it. I think the record for her waiting was about 7 minutes. By this time, we had nearly finished our first course and were ready and waiting to ask for seconds. Poor Aunt Marama was still there with her hands in her lap waiting for one of the family to notice and pass her whatever it was she was waiting for, and her meal was pretty cold by this time.

Aunt Marama was an amazing woman. Her honesty and integrity could never be questioned, and she was always consistent.

Some of my Mum's gripes were knives and forks being waved around in the air while eating, talking with your mouth full, or leaving the table before anyone else had finished. For these three, I have to agree with her.

The consequences of not leaving the table before everyone had finished did not establish itself until my children came along. Like most small children, they wanted to leave the table as quickly as possible once they'd eaten. They were desperate to get back to playing whichever game they had been engrossed in before being 'rudely interrupted' to come to the table for dinner in the first place. Meals were just a refuelling point for them.

As a way to entice the children to stay, I started to tell made up stories about random things that came into my head. I had a vivid imagination, so storytelling was pretty easy. The kids loved it, and most nights, I was asked to tell a story.

When the kids were a little older, stories morphed into general knowledge questions. They had to answer questions on a general world subject.

Claire used to infuriate her brothers by never remembering where the Sea of Tranquility was or the height of Mount Everest, even though it may have been asked a dozen times in the previous six months.

They would roll their eyes and make all sorts of noises in frustration as Claire sat there, dumbfounded yet again, with a blank look on her face, trying hard to recall this small fact.

We all laugh about that these days because the answers are now forever ingrained in her memory.

Michael said a few years ago, the reason he often cleans up in pub quizzes is because of those family quizzes as he grew up.

While seeing no relevance or point at the time, he now realises how much knowledge he learnt and retained from those nightly dining table quizzes.

Even today, he has superb general knowledge and amazing recall of the smallest of facts. I think he has won quite a bit of money at quiz competitions as a result of his general knowledge. Unfortunately, he has never shared any of the proceeds with me!

When you sit around the dining table with your kids, discuss the best thing about their day or the challenge they had for that day. You get a deeper understanding of what is happening in their lives. Best of all, the children see Mum and Dad taking a real interest in them and how they are getting on in life.

These are the times when you can have the hard conversations, and the family will open up and help each other.

Our dinners sometimes lasted up to an hour or so with quizzes, stories or chats about life and living.

A fool-proof way to get your kids to respond

How often have you tried to connect with or contact your children through every social medium they use, with no reply? Is it frustrating? It was for me.

A trick I learnt was to write a letter to them. Amongst other things, I stated in the letter that I was enclosing $50 because I knew it would help them. I didn't actually enclose the money though.

If you do this, I can almost guarantee you will get a response from them within an hour of them receiving the letter. Make sure you cover all the points you want to talk about, before talking about the $50 that wasn't enclosed.

Going a little too far

Claire was about three years old, and I was having a bit of fun with her. I was niggling her repeatedly. She asked me to stop but I carried on, and my fun turned into a source of annoyance for her. She finally reacted by spitting in my face. That brought the household to a standstill. The boys fell about with laughter, Claire stared straight at me, and my wife simply reminded me that Claire had tried to warn me.

The great lesson I learnt here was that when teaching our children about boundaries, we need to set an example and respect their boundaries too. Spitting at me, was the only way left for Claire to get my 'attention' and get me to stop annoying her. And she did! I learnt a valuable lesson that day about respecting my children's boundaries.

Backyard cricket

Michael was an amazing child. He was absolutely sporting mad. Anything that resembled a ball, he would kick, pass, play with or throw. Anything resembling a bat, he would pick up to hit a ball, coconut, orange, apple or anything else he could find.

Our backyard was often used as an impromptu cricket pitch where Michael would play for hours with his friends. Of course, we had broken windows, broken bats, broken wickets and even some broken bones as well.

Sporting events require energy which tends to bring on hunger of magnificent proportions in young boys. Our dining room table had its fair share of use by our children, their friends and hangers-on, all constantly vying for the food that seemed to be forever available to them.

The chairs had slats at the back that looked like cricket wickets. I came home one day from work and saw that three of the chairs had the slats busted clean out from the back of them.

Michael, along with three of his friends were looking very sheepish and trying to avoid the subject of the damaged chairs.

Michael has always been incredibly honest, so I asked him straight; "Michael, what happened to the chairs?"

He lifted his head, looked me directly in the eye and said; "Dad, we used them as cricket wickets because our real ones got busted so we had to substitute. But Dad, you should have seen the way the ball shattered them when it got through the batsmen. Just like on TV".

I could not help but laugh. The chairs couldn't be fixed, so it gave us a good excuse to go and buy a new set of dining room furniture. Of course, we gave very strict instructions that no chairs from this dining room set were ever to be used as cricket wickets.

Rules for young adults

Our children had boundaries and rules that they could measure themselves against as they grew up. You may agree or disagree with the rules we had. Emulate them all if you wish or choose some parts and discard others. All I ask is that you have some rules that your children can follow and live by. You will be better off and richer for it and so will they.

As our children were growing into young adults, we suggested and guided them to follow these simple rules:

1. **Think, speak and act like an adult if you want to be treated like one**

   "Step Up" to more responsibilities. If you do, your parents will "Step Aside" and give you more freedom.

2. **Stay out of trouble and don't be where trouble is**

   Nothing good happens after midnight. The later it gets, the more likely you're hanging with drunk, bored and angry people looking for danger.

3. **Don't wish your problems were smaller or that life was easier**

   Instead, grow yourself and increase your ability to deal with real life. Put good things into your head by what you read, what you watch, what you listen to and by the games you play.

4. **Strive to become competitive with good character**

   Strut your stuff but develop your character along the way so you can be proud of the person you are. Be humble.

5. **Don't let success go to your head nor failure to your heart**

   Life is a series of wins and losses and often both simultaneously. Treat success and failure as temporary and neither will take you off course.

6. **Sex without commitment is like tomato sauce without a pie**

   Build your relationship as if in a slow cooker, not a microwave, so you don't become emotionally burnt out and romantically used up.

Rules for parents

As we did for our children, we also set rules for ourselves, and in each of my marriages, I have tried to abide by these rules.

1. **Love intentionally and not just emotionally**

   Visualise your kids as adults, successful in their work and happy in their personal lives. In 25-30 years, your children will be running the world. They could be making decisions for you.

2. **Be fair, clear and put it in writing**

   Take the opportunity while your kids are dependent on you to prepare them to live away from home. Involve them in the running of the home. Contribution brings ownership, pride and confidence.

3. **Be an effective parenting unit**

   Most parents were raised differently from each another and yet are expected to parent from the same page. About half of parents don't live under the same roof. Nonetheless, sticking together is still the best way to show love.

4. **Move from control to influence and from nurturing to empowering**

   Micro-manage less, expect more. Let kids feel the consequences of their actions. Help in a dangerous situation but let them develop their own wisdom.

5. **Keep track of the money they owe you**

   Don't give your kids money just to keep the peace. Encourage them to get a part-time job and learn to live on a budget.

Unintended consequences

Louisa is my stepdaughter, and I had been in her life for around four years when she was a 19-year-old on her gap year in England. She was enjoying herself and understanding what the world was like outside the small town of Blenheim, New Zealand.

Michael, my son, was completing his last year at Fairfield University in Connecticut USA, where he had obtained a football scholarship and was studying sporting media.

He had a football graduation ceremony coming up that I was going to attend. I was taking about two weeks beforehand to do a bit of a road trip around the Eastern seaboard of the USA, to see the US Civil War sites.

Louisa heard about this and wanted to join me. She said she was going to fly from England to travel with me to Michael's graduation.

I was taken aback by this and talked with Janelle, saying to her; "this is not right. I can't travel alone with my 19-year-old stepdaughter".

Janelle asked me, "How come?"

I needed guidance on this issue, so I spoke with my pastor, Ali. He asked; "Who has the issue?".

I said; "Me. My beautiful, lovely 19-year-old step-daughter wants to travel with me. We will be staying in the same hotels or motels together".

He asked; "What is the issue? She obviously trusts you enough to suggest it".

I then went and saw my other pastor friend, Lawrence, from another church to get his perspective. I needed the perspective and guidance of two trusted advisors. Lawrence asked me; "Who has the issue here?"

Two pastors were saying the same thing. Janelle, my wife, just smiled at me and said; "Louisa trusts you like her father. Go and enjoy your time with her." So I did, and we had the most incredible time together.

There was also an unintended consequence to this trip. Louisa saw what Michael was achieving and said to me; "Dad, I want some of this. I see what Michael is doing, what he is achieving, and I want to come to the States to do my University study. I was drifting before, but I see so clearly now what I want to do".

We sat in a 'Ruby Tuesday' diner, somewhere on the east coast of the USA and planned out her next move and how she was going to get into a US University on scholarship. She wrote her plan and set her goal, just like I'd shown her previously. There were milestones to achieve along the way.

A year later, Louisa had been admitted to West Virginia University on a full Rowing Scholarship. She graduated four years later as an Industrial Engineer, with a 4.0 GPA. The unintended consequences of small things.

John Anderson says; "Some parents give their children every material thing they desire and shower them with money. Young people have to earn and learn the value of money. Give it all to them, and you have taken away their incentive. Give them love and encouragement, and they will achieve, often way above their wildest dreams".

My learnings:

- [x] Correct parenting is one of the hardest job descriptions I have ever been given
- [x] Children need boundaries to work between and butt up against; it makes them feel safe
- [x] Time spent with family around the dining room table is precious

Your learnings:

- [ ]
- [ ]
- [ ]

#1 Engine - Goal Setting

After an A380 take-off, other planes have to wait up to three minutes before they can start their take-off, due to wake turbulence from its four massive engines and wingtips. During the flight, other aircraft must remain at least 20km behind "in trail," to ensure they don't get caught in the wing vortexes or engine wake turbulence of the A380.

Waiting allows us to make proper decisions in business and family. Looking forward into the distance to see what is ahead, and from afar, allows us to see potential mistakes or issues before they happen. This allows us to adjust our course before we make a mistake. Being emotional can lead to bad decision-making. Waiting three minutes takes the heat out of a situation and allows for calm and logical responses.

Michael and goal setting

Michael started playing football with his brother when he was four years old. The other boys on the team were five or six years old. Michael showed a natural ability early on and often ran circles around his taller and older opposition. He went on to become a particularly adept striker. Most seasons he would be scoring northward of 40 or more goals.

He came to his mother and me when he was in his early teens and inexplicably said; "I'm going to switch to be a goalkeeper."

I was shocked. I could not understand why. From my perspective, he had the skills to progress to the highest levels as a football striker.

Michael saw it differently; "I'm not fast enough or agile enough to make it to the higher echelons of elite football".

With that, in what I thought was a very bad decision, he switched to goalie.

Little did I realise that this switch would propel him to the pinnacle of his sporting career, representing New Zealand as a goalkeeper at the 2012 Olympics.

Aged 13, he had the vision to see what I could not see. He had the strength of character, determination and tenacity to make the change, then practice and learn his trade to become a world-class goalie. He was determined to make himself the absolute best he could.

He set himself a checklist of achievements that he had to complete to make it to the top. This started with making the NZ age-grade teams at under 15's, under 17's and under 19's level, before being selected for the Olympics. Michael was considering his end goal.

He had the end-goal in mind.

Every person and business needs a vision:

- What does the end goal look like?
- Start with the end in mind.
- What are the milestones you need to achieve to get there.
- Who do I need to BE to get there

In the absence of clearly defined goals, we are forced to concentrate on activity and ultimately become enslaved to it. If goal-scoring were taken out of a game of football, you'd have 22 players running around aimlessly and no need for a referee.

Jason Fried, in his great book, 'Rework', describes the beginning:

"The stuff you have to do is where you should begin. Start at the epicentre. For example, if you open a hot dog stand, you can worry about the cart, the name, or the decoration. But the first thing you should worry about is the hot dog. The hot dog is the epicentre".

The way to find the epicentre is to ask the question:

If I took this away, would what I am selling still exist?

Figure out the epicentre. What part of the equation can't be removed? If you continue to get away without things, they aren't the epicentre. When you find it, you'll know.

If I took you to Paddington train station in London and put you on a train, what is the first question you will ask me?

"Where am I going?"

If you don't know where you're going, it doesn't matter what train you get on, or where you end up.

You need to know where you're going so you get on the right train, going to the right destination. This is your Vision; the end goal.

Every person needs a list of stepping stones (the milestones) to get to the result they desire. We often do this in business but not for our personal circumstances. Apply it to your family as well. You'll be a better person for it.

I should have applied these principles to my marriage, my family and personal situation. It is too easy to go into a relationship without understanding what the end goal looks like. The focus is on the wedding day or moving in together, without looking at what the end picture should look like – the marriage.

Brad Sugars jokingly says in his seminars, that people spend weeks, months, and even years planning a wedding, and yet they spend absolutely zero minutes planning a marriage. While he says this in a joking fashion, there is a real serious element to his statement.

That's why people can have amazing weddings and crappy marriages. What planning goes into a marriage?

Start asking questions;

How many times each week are we going to spend time just by ourselves?

What interests are we going to spend time on regularly?

What are the top five things we enjoy doing together?

When you go into business, you go and read a dozen books on how to succeed in business. You read books on planning, on sales and marketing, you go and read all of that.

When you get into a relationship or marriage, how many books do you read on having a good relationship?

That's just crazy. You can't start a relationship without any learning whatsoever on how to be in a relationship. If you're not reading at least one book a year on marriage or on having a better relationship, don't expect it to get any better.

Having a vision isn't enough; there has to be a commitment to act on it. That's called a mission, and it requires setting specific, measurable steps to achieve it. Those steps are called goals. They establish a plan for accomplishing your mission and thus fulfilling your vision.

You'll generally have one vision but many goals. And each goal you reach brings you a step closer to fulfilling your vision

You've got to learn the techniques of it. You've got to learn the skills of making a great relationship work.

Do you do behavioural profiling with your family? In business, people do DISC profiles or communication profiles or Myers Briggs profiles with their staff. Yet, they go home and think it is not necessary for the most important journey they will undertake, a journey even more important than their business.

Why wouldn't you do that at home and make sure you know who your spouse or partner is, and what profile your kids have so you can communicate in their language style so that you can understand their behaviour and their decision-making profiles?

All of these are simple things we don't do in our relationships. If you just applied the lessons of business to your family, you'd probably get a lot better at family as well.

The Power of having a Written Goal:

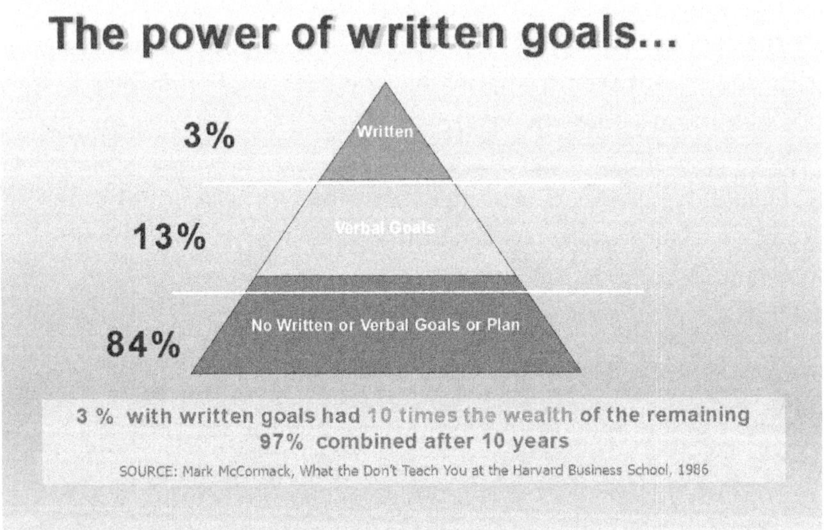

A fascinating study was done at Harvard in 1986. They took a group of students and asked them, who had written gaols. Only 3% of the students had written goals out of the whole class. 84% said they had no written or verbal goals. 13% admitted to having verbal goals, but they weren't written anywhere.

10 years later the researchers went back to this group of students. They found that the 3% who had written their goals all those years ago, actually had 10 times the wealth of the rest of the 97% put together.

This is how powerful having written visual goals are. Don't underestimate the power of your own written goals. When you have a desire to achieve a certain goal and it is written down with a time frame attached to it, it is incredibly powerful and motivational.

Your goals should be stretching and not easily attainable. It must have an air of uncertainty in achieving it. You need to stretch yourself, and this stretching builds perseverance and sustainability.

Then next time when you push for your next goal you will search for one that is just a little more difficult than the previous goal. This stretching helps you build your future, and not be put off by the first obstacle you're confronted by. You will persevere more than before to achieve this new goal.

'Write the vision and make it plain.' Habakkuk 2:2 NKJV

When people have no vision for the future, they tend to do three things:

- Revert to their past
- Spend all their time making excuses for why their lives are going nowhere
- Stop living and settle for mere existence.

Take on board the Chindit's Motto when you look to your future: *The boldest methods are the safest. This means go at the problem and say sorry later.*

If the first plan you adopt does not work successfully, replace it with a new plan. If this plan fails to work, replace it with a new plan and another until you find one that works. There are no unsuccessful goals, only timeframes. Most people who meet with failure do so because of their lack of persistence in creating new plans to take the place of those which fail. Temporary defeat should mean only one thing; the certain knowledge that there is something wrong with the plan.

Human nature is such that unless you have a clear picture of your future, you will always return to your past.

If you don't keep score, how do you know who's winning?

It's important to keep score, so you know how you're progressing along the roadway of life. If you don't keep score, then you have no benchmark with which to adjust what you're achieving.

Why do all sports teams keep score? If we didn't keep score, what would be the point of the game? What would be achieved?

In football, if you didn't keep score, how would you know who won. With no score-keeping, you may revert to deciding who has the best pair of legs and award them the win. Would that work?

It is the same in business. You must keep score. Otherwise, you won't know how solvent your business is.

A business dashboard

So how do you keep score in business? Let me explain. Would you drive your car without a dashboard giving you vital information like fuel state, speed and temperature reading? If I asked you to rip out the dashboard of your car and drive without it, would you?

Have a dashboard in your business as well. Keep score of your cash flow, turnover, profit, customer base and orders. Pick the key areas that need to be measured in your business, so you keep track of your business's vital statistics.

A friend of mine in the plumbing trade measures how much fuel his fleet of 17 vans use every week. The drivers know he is

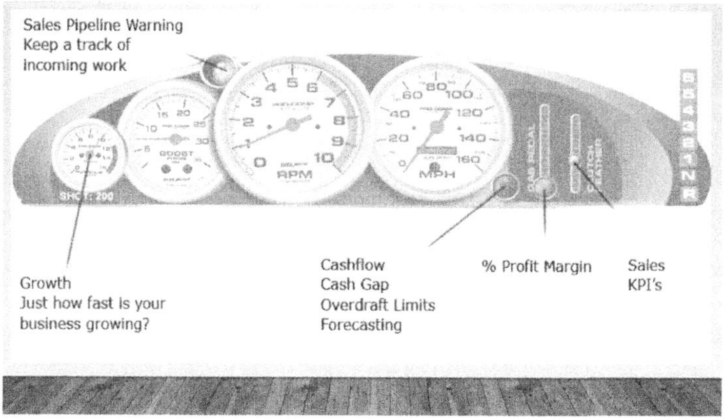

measuring this, and they are now aware of their driving habits and how it can impact on fuel economy. They also know they can't go for 'jollies' on the bosses fuel card. Just this one vital measurement has saved the company a staggering £57,000 in fuel bills every year. What gets measured, gets done.

A story about goal setting

Ben was in his last year at school. He had been in France the year before on an AFS (American Field Scholarship) student exchange scholarship. He had come home early to try and become head boy at his college.

He succeeded in this endeavour and was now looking to head off to Otago University to study medicine.

Ben wanted to continue his rugby career. He was a good player but would only ever be a journeyman in the game. As you've already read in this book, I suggested he became a rugby referee. I had refereed for 24 years and thoroughly enjoyed it.

The first year of medical school is incredibly difficult, and if Ben injured himself playing rugby, it could jeopardise his medical career. Being a referee meant that Ben would remain involved in the game and, if he was good enough, the NZRFU would fly him around the country refereeing games on the weekend, which would be a great release from his studies.

Ben thought about this and started refereeing. Along with his medical studies, he set himself goals each year to progress his refereeing career. Those goals were printed up where he could see them.

Ben had goals for his medical career and his refereeing career. He realised the importance of having them both aligned. He could do one without the other, but that was not his intention.

Being 6'4", and having a lovely demeanour, helped him with his game management and to see over rucks, mauls and scrums and identify nefarious player infractions. Having the ability to run the 100m in about 10 seconds, enabled him to keep up with the quickest of wingers.

Ben moved from club games to refereeing provincial games. This propelled him to refereeing the under 20 world cup final, before moving into super rugby and finally tier one rugby test matches. He was the youngest international rugby referee of his time.

When he was 29 years of age, Ben was a successful Doctor of Medicine specialising in Ophthalmology. He had also built a successful rugby refereeing career.

He checked off the goals he had achieved on his list and realised he completed all he had set out to do earlier than expected.

This is the power of setting goals.

If you take nothing else away from this book, start writing down your goals and keep them handy. Look at them often. Just this one small act will drive you further than you ever thought possible.

I use many acronyms for goal setting because some resonate, and some don't. I want to give you a sample, so you can choose what works for you.

Remember, you are a human and an individual. You are a Human Being, not a Human Doing. The way you perceive the world will be different from your peers, your family and your friends. The way you achieve goals will also be different. Use the acronym that works best for you.

Do you have a dream chart?

A dream chart is a way of putting on a board the things you want to achieve over a given period. Pictures are great as it helps you visualise what you want to achieve and the results you want to get.

As I have already alluded to, pictures are better than words because our mind works in pictures. You should have a mixture of personal and business dreams and goals. People often have goals that are often only business related. This is an incorrect way of doing things as we'll discuss shortly.

Here is a great example of a dream board a friend of ours made up. It's colourful, it has pictures, it has time frames, and each month they tick off what they have achieved. They also acknowledge what they haven't achieved and talk about the reason it didn't happen.

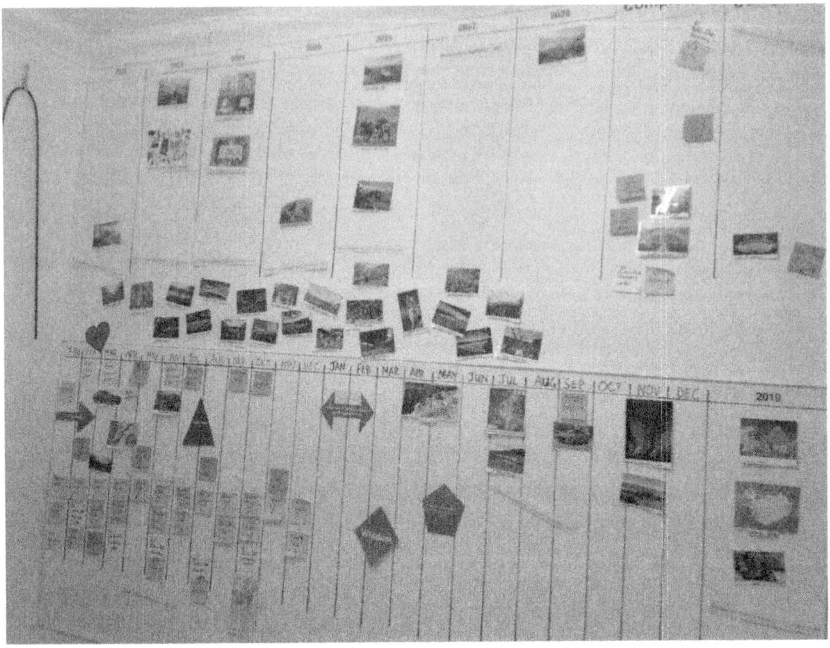

This is on the wall of their office, so they see it every day.

If you have a dream chart or a bucket list, most of the things on there are private and family oriented. But when you ask a business owner for their goals, it immediately morphs into business-related goals, and there is nothing personal there. They don't have goals that are family or travel related or time-off related.

I often ask a Business owner; "What are your ideal number of hours working per week?"

And they reply; "Oh, less than I'm doing." That's not an actual goal. Is your goal to work five hours a day, four days a week or is your goal to work eight hours a day, five days a week?

A formula for success

dreams x goals x learning x plans x action = success

What's your actual goal? What's the number that you're shooting for?

Not many people set these things. It's hard to get people to plan for it. A lot of the time, it comes down to a very simple thing. People don't plan. They let working **IN** the business get in the way of everything.

The challenge with any business is there's always 500 things to do today. And guess how many things there are going to be tomorrow? 500 things. And guess how many there are going to be the day after that? 500 things to do.

It doesn't matter how many you cross off your list; the next day there's still another 500 things to do. That's just the nature of business, so you've got to **prioritise** what is important.

Remember: **Accept** you will never be able to do everything you want because there is just too much to do. Prioritise the important ones.

If a business cannot work without you being there, it is not a business. It's a job, and you work for the craziest person in the world.

You go from working for one crazy business owner when you were employed, to working for an even worse one when you're self-employed: yourself.

When you start a business, you plan and set goals. When you get into a relationship or a marriage, you don't make any goals or plans. You just sort of fall into it and go along, hoping it's going to be all right. Goal setting is that important. That is why I have repeatedly stressed the importance throughout this book.

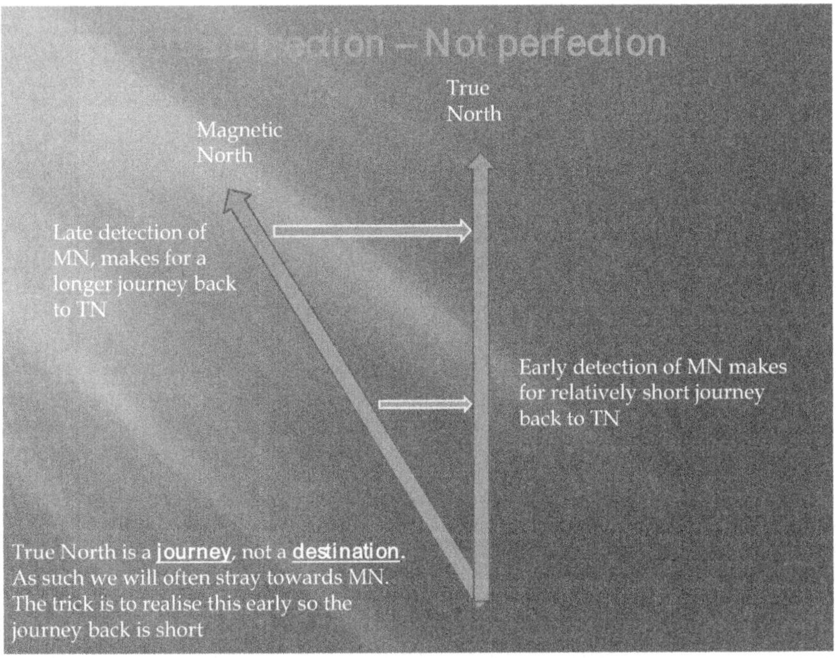

You are on a journey, and you need direction, not perfection. Any goal you set gives you direction. You are heading for True North. Each time you head off to Magnetic North you are off-piste; you have lost direction. You are off your goal. The longer you journey on Magnetic North, the longer it takes you to get back to True North. Early detection of you being off-goal means it is easier to get back on track. Like the taps on your highway of life, don't wait for it to be too late to change.

To be successful, a business needs both a spiritual and business mission. When a business gets too big, it forgets its mission, or if the mission it was created for, is no longer needed, then the business begins to die. The mission of a business should fill a need that the clients want and if it fills that need, and fills it well, the business will prosper.

We can identify the mission of someone who is trying to sell us something for a commission, as contrasted to someone trying to help answer our needs.

Many businesses will never get what they desire because they forget their mission and stop fulfilling the needs of their customers. If you continually look at and review your spiritual and business mission, people will say it is something that your business does and has always done. There will never be a variation away from what you set out to do because you are focused on the direction you have taken. People want to deal with business owners who have a very credible business.

Let's look at some goal setting techniques and acronyms.

S.M.A.R.T and S.M.A.R.T.E.R

One you have probably heard of is **S.M.A.R.T.** goals.

These are

Specific

Measurable

Achievable

Realistic

Timely

Let's use the example of, "*I want to lose weight.*"

This is **A**chievable and probably **R**ealistic. Lose 1lb, and we have achieved the goal.

But it is not **S**pecific, **M**easurable or **T**imely. It is not a S.M.A.R.T goal.

What about setting a goal to "*lose 20lbs?*"

Now we have something **S**pecific, **M**easurable, **A**chievable, maybe **R**ealistic but not **T**imely.

How about a goal to "*lose 20lb in the next two weeks?*"

Now we have a goal that is **S**pecific, **M**easurable, and **T**imely. However, it is not **R**ealistic or **A**chievable to lose that amount of weight in such a short period of time.

How about aiming to "*lose 20lb of weight in the next 120 days*"?

Now we have something **S**pecific that we can **M**easure on a daily/weekly basis that is **A**chievable, **R**ealistic and **T**imely.

I want to add **E.R.** on to our goals to make them **S.M.A.R.T.E.R** goals.

Emotion
Reward

These two extra letters or words give us extra meaning and desire to achieving our S.M.A.R.T. goal.

Let's look at Emotion and Reward in our losing weight example.

What is the Emotion you will feel as you see the weight dropping off? What will it feel like when people notice your loss of weight and comment on how good you look?

What **R**eward will you give yourself at the end of 120 days when 20lb has vanished? Make it something that contributes to your success, not a large chocolate cake. Something like a new pair of jeans, or the dress you have had your eye on.

Goal setting – again

Claire was an excellent dancer. She loved Highland and Irish. Being the youngest child, she went to her brothers and asked them to help her set some goals. I recall overhearing the conversation. Both boys were incredibly supportive, letting Claire know how good she was at dancing. They asked her what she desired. She said she wanted to be NZ dance champion in her age group. They asked her when she wanted to achieve this. She replied, 'in two years.

They then asked her what she needed to 'DO' to achieve this. She rattled off the list of things she needed to do, such as practice four times a week for 1.5 hours each time, and having the right diet, and exercising properly.

They then asked her what she needed to 'BE' to achieve her goal. Now Claire was flummoxed. The boys helped her with this, and Claire realised she needed to be goal and result orientated. She needed to be passionate and driven. Each week she needed an incremental increase in her output and performance to get her to her desired outcome.

After a couple of hours and lots of scribbles and notes, Claire had her plan. Two years later Claire was age grade dance champion, and she had great delight in ticking off her goal as 'mission achieved.'

What I see happen is that people only set business goals. If you only set goals in business, then you're not going to have health, because you don't have any health goals. If you don't have any relationship goals, how will you ensure your relationship remains on track? It's not just your relationship with your spouse or partner; it's the relationship with your kids. It's all those things.

If you sit down and look at it, what is your goal with your kids? Is your goal to invest an hour a day with them? Is your goal to invest an hour a day with your spouse or partner?

Your family is a team, so what is your goal for the team?

Where is the team headed? What is the team aiming to achieve?

A lot of the time, people don't understand what it is they're aiming to achieve with their family. There's no goal for it. We invest time into business goals but not as much time into our own personal and family goals.

With the business, there's a goal to make X number of dollars and build the business to that point. With the family, often enough, you don't have goals decided or a vision for the family as to; "What are we trying to achieve?"

By not having a goal, it's easy to get distracted from it because the area where you do have a goal, you put in the time, energy and effort.

Patton said it brilliantly when he reiterated; "*An average plan executed now with violence, is better than a perfect plan executed next week.*"

Know what your true north is and how to keep away from magnetic north. If you stray onto magnetic north, get back on your correct path as quickly as possible. Execute your plan now, don't wait for it to be perfect.

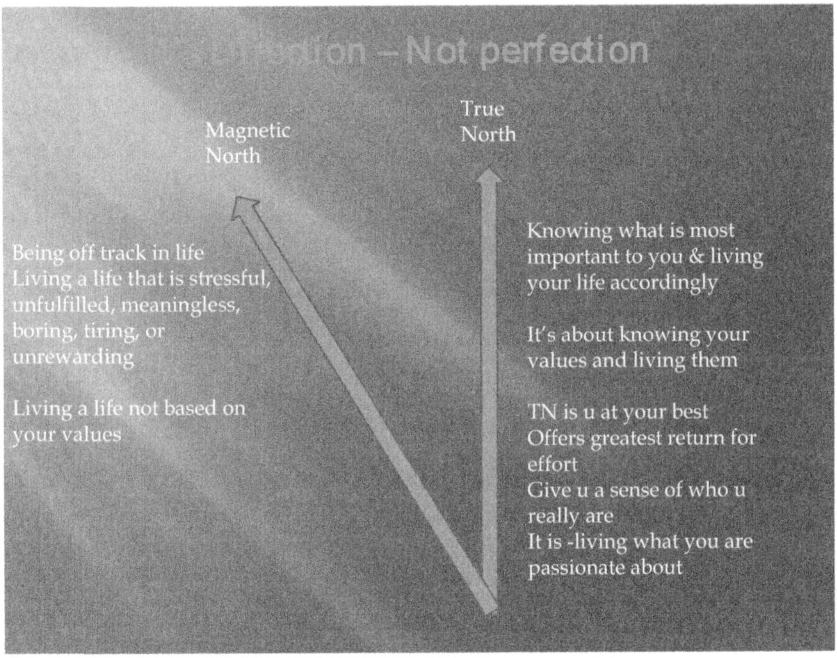

my learnings:

- [x] I must find the epicentre of my business – nothing else matters before this
- [x] I must have personal, family and relationship goals, not just business goals
- [x] S.M.A.R.T.E.R. goals with Emotion and Reward brings about change more quickly

Your learnings:

- [ ]
- [ ]
- [ ]

I would like to share another acronym with you to help you journey forward to reach your desired goal. I have used this quite often to help people understand how to take some action.

S.U.C.C.E.S.S.

Success is a progressive realisation of a **worthy ideal**. A **worthy ideal** is something you love with a passion. You have to have a vision of what you want to be.

S.U.C.C.E.S.S. is an acronym for:

Set goals

Understand why you want what you want

Commit action to it

Contemplate other possibilities

Evaluate where you are compared to the goal

Stickability- don't give up

Surrender to questions- it directs your focus. Are you achieving?

If you're not chasing your dream, you're already dead.

If failure wasn't an option, what would you do, be, or have? What could you achieve? Try D.O.N.E. as another formula for goal setting.

D.O.N.E.

Discover values Where have they come from? Values motivate and evaluate. Labels I give myself that are important to me.

Order What's important to me right now?

- mindset
- self-belief
- being congruent

Needs

Certainty in Life	–	faith, facts, routine, control.
Uncertainty in life	–	drama, new relationships, new locations
Significance	–	style and looks, material possessions
Love and Connection	–	spirituality, pets, partners, growth contribution

Evaluate

Question things

Ask good questions - get good answers

Attachment - I came into the world alone, and I will go alone. I am having a spiritual experience in a human body.

Questions direct your focus

B.S.Q.A.S.H.

This formula was developed in 2000 by the German Football Federation. They had just been beaten in the first round of the European Cup that year. The nation was despondent and reeling from the loss.

In desperation, the German football governing body sat down to formulate a plan to win the Football World Cup in 2014.

This is the goal setting formula they used to put that plan into action.

Big What is the big desire you want to achieve?

Specific goal is better than a broad goal

Quick - move

Any goal is better than no goal

Small steps but with milestones to measure progress

Hard goal is better than an easy goal

Within three months, they had their blueprint formulated and ready to roll out amongst the Bundesliga and focusing on the six-year-old + players. Six years old and above were the players in 14 years' time (aged 20 +) who would win them the world cup.

And guess what, that is exactly what they went on to achieve. The nation was back on top of the footballing world.

W.A.V.E. A.S. G.O.D.

How about waving to God to give you inspiration for your goal setting? Here is another formula, given to me by my friend Tosin.

The Goal

Write it down. Write it daily. You may have heard that it takes 30 days to embed a habit, but it takes 90 days for the discipline to be instilled. It takes 90 days to install the discipline to achieve the goal. If you miss one day, then you have to start again.

Attention- Focus on it. Give the goal the attention it needs.

Visualisation- A butterfly can't see its wings but everyone else can. Butterfly wings are not for them; they are for everyone else to see. Visualise your goal.

Energy- Give it water. Give it life. Let it grow inside of you.

Affirmation - Your incantation sheet. Verbalise to yourself every day, with emotion, the goal you desire.

Sowing- Give to the universe. It has provided for you, so give back to the Universe.

Gratitude- Be grateful for everything you have.

Ownership- Own what you desire and be accountable and responsible for making it happen.

Detachment- Don't worry about how. Be open to how. Know what you want. Get out of the way. Let your God or your universe help you make it happen.

A powerful mechanism I have learnt is **Autosuggestion**.

Autosuggestion is what you suggest to the universe. You throw it out there. Be specific about what you want. Feel it. Have the emotions coursing through your body. Taste it. See it happening and continue to autosuggest it to the universe and see the results that occur.

My learnings:

- [x] My success is down to learning each day
- [x] Gratitude is something I must practice every day in both business and my personal relationship with my family
- [x] Asking good questions enables me to get great answers

Your learnings:

- [ ]
- [ ]
- [ ]

Vision

Goal setting is your long-term vision. Start with the end in mind. This will bring clarity to your journey and focus you on the milestones you need to achieve to get to your absolute end goal. The stepping stones along the pathway to the end.

A vision puts you on a mission, and a contagious spirit can be felt, causing you to rise and drive toward your goal.

Helen Keller said it wonderfully when she said: "What would be worse than being blind? **To have sight but with no vision**".

What an amazing statement from a blind woman.

Vision:

1st Horizon Wanderers	–	never see it
2nd Horizon Followers	–	never pursue it on their own
3rd Horizon Achievers	–	see it and pursue it
4th Horizon Influencers	–	see it, pursue it and help others do the same

We all live under the same sky, but we all have different horizons.

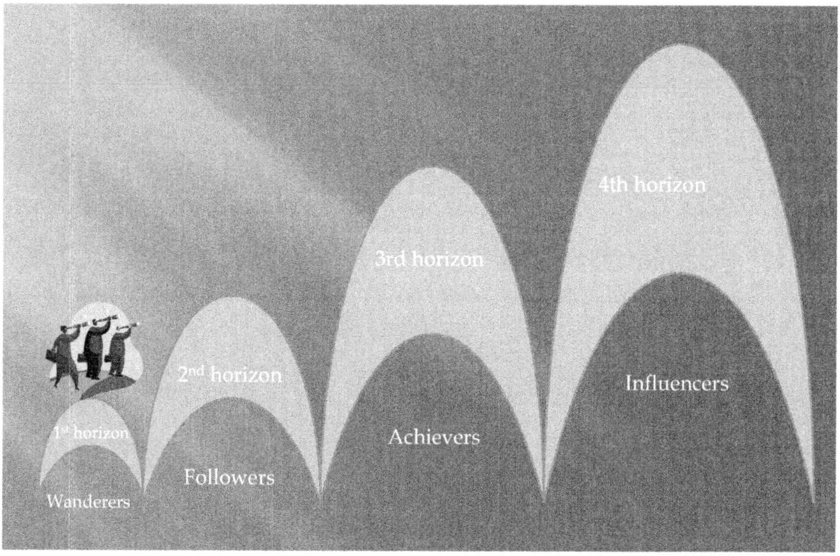

1st horizon We can't see it and wander around looking for it. We change jobs often and never see what an organisation can do for us, or us for the organisation.

2nd horizon We are highly motivated, but we need someone to get us to the top to show us the view and the next horizon.

3rd horizon Success is sensed by these people. They want to get to the next horizon because they can see it, sense it and feel it. They need direction and guidance to get to that next horizon and will keep going.

4th horizon Nothing gets in the way. They are focused. No excuses. They are accountable to themselves. They want to do what they can. Each horizon is just another challenge to beat and get on top of. This is the land of the legend.

- You must have absolute belief that you can do this
- You must accept the opportunities that come your way and ensure you see the 4th horizon
- You must accept the knocks and difficulties that come with building a business and relationship. Keep focused on the horizon. When things go wrong, (as they do in life) if you keep concentrating on your vision and goals, it removes the negativity. You can't have negative goals.

A story

An East Coast Bishop paid a visit to a Midwestern religious college. He stayed at the home of the college president, who served as a professor of physics and chemistry.

During a discussion after dinner, the Bishop declared that just about everything had been discovered and all inventions conceived.

The young college president politely disagreed and said he felt there would be many more discoveries. When the Bishop challenged the president to name just one such invention, the president replied that he was certain that within fifty years men would be able to fly.

"Nonsense!" was the only reply the Bishop could sputter. "Only angels were intended to fly."

The Bishop's name was Wright, and he had two boys at home who may have lived under the same sky but had different horizons. Their names were Orville and Wilbur Wright.

A vision is simply **an imaginative insight**, at a specific point in time, about the future. It is a signpost for all who work in your team, helping them to understand what the organisation is and where it intends to go.

Is it possible for a business owner to influence the engagement of a group of employees either singularly or as a group?

Is it possible for a person to influence their family so they can work together in harmony and understand what everyone in the family desires and wants to achieve?

If you have an ambitious vision, you will put capital and resources into the business or relationship and carry the risk. Not everyone will have a similar ambition. That's OK. But this vision will not be achieved unless everyone in your sphere of influence is ambitious and wants to get to the far horizon.

To mine an ounce of gold, what must you do?

Go looking for the gold. You will probably move several tons of dirt to get that ounce of gold. But you didn't go mining for dirt; you went mining for gold. Always dig through the dirt to find that nugget.

Don't plan for today, plan for tomorrow and keep looking for opportunities to find gold. Achieve your goals and influence others in your peer group.

It won't be easy, and you will be shifting a lot of dirt to reach your end point. There will be a lot of emotion. However, the reward and complete sense of satisfaction at the other end will be like a drug. You'll want some more of it. Therefore, set another goal and make that work.

Imagine setting a goal of getting £5000 in your savings account by the end of the year. Your stepping stone is to put £100 away every week. Small but achievable goals. What is the emotion you will feel as you see your bank balance rising?

A story

I was working with a client who ran a small printing business. Let's call him 'Warren'. It was his dream to go to Vienna with his wife for a week's holiday, but he had never achieved this. I asked Warren how much he would need for flights, accommodation, food and sightseeing.

He knew exactly because he had worked it out and updated it every year; £3,800. It was a goal he desired but didn't know how to achieve. £3,800 was just too much to try and obtain. He had thought of going to the bank to get a loan.

I asked Warren when he would like to go. He said; "In November, in nine months' time."

"What's stopping you?" I asked him.

Warren replied; "I can never save that amount of money".

"OK," I replied. "Let's break it down. You have nine months to get £3,800. How much is that per month, and per week?"

He worked it out; "£422 per month; £97 per week".
"How achievable is that?" I asked.

He couldn't believe it. "Very achievable," Warren said. He had never broken it down like this before.

"Go home and tell your wife what you are going to do," I told him.

"Why?" he asked. "I want to surprise her."

I suggested to him, two reasons. "Firstly, this is about accountability. If you tell your wife, you will be committed, so you don't let her down. Secondly, I think you'll find it fun to do this together."

"OK,"' replied Warren a little hesitantly.

I went on to say, "I want you to make up a wallchart together with a weekly and monthly timeline with £97 put in each week and £422 every month. Get some pictures of Vienna and some pictures of the things you want to see and do there, restaurants you want to visit, sights you want to see. Pick the airline you want to fly with. Put all these on what we will call your 'dream board' and put it somewhere where you will both see it every day. As part of the accountability process, you will need to update me at every coaching session as to how the goal is progressing".

Nine months later, Warren and his wife flew off to Vienna with £4,300 in their pocket. This was after they had paid for their flights. They did have a blip on weeks 17 and 18, due to a debtor not paying as required. This was quickly sorted, and they recovered to put extra away.

Warren and his wife were astounded to see how quickly the money started to build up by taking small steps. They were amazed. By focusing their attention on what they desired, the universe had helped them for the first time in their life, do something they had always wanted to do. Since then Warren has gone on to run a very successful business, with a nice lifestyle. He continues to set goals, with milestones and will often send me a picture of his new dream-chart.

Vienna will always remain the starting point of their new life.

Warren now understands you need a dream and a vision to understand that there is "gold" amongst all the dirt, and you must go digging for it, to make it happen.

- Do you have a dream for your future?
- Have you shared it with anyone?
- What happens if you fail?
- Failure is a critical step to success. Get up, dust yourself off and move on.
- More importantly, what happens when you succeed?

Care and respect: Action Plan

Major attributes you need for Change and Goal setting:

- Unwavering courage
- Self-control
- A keen sense of justice
- Definiteness of decision
- Definiteness of plans
- The habit of doing more than paid for
- A pleasing personality
- Sympathy and understanding
- Mastery of detail
- Willingness to assume full responsibility
- Cooperation

How to stop kids from using their tech at the dinner table

Have you ever had your children be so distant from you at the dinner table because they are playing on their iPhone or iPad? Many kids think their throat is cut if they are away from their technology for more than five minutes.

Janelle and I developed a little strategy to sort this small dilemma out. We had the children put all smartphones and iPads into the middle of the table at dinner time. Whoever reached for their phone if it rung or pinged, had to do the table clearing and dishes that night.

You'll find that after about a week, nobody dares reach for the phone. Friends start to realise as well, don't ring or text because it is dinner time in the O'Keeffe household and nobody will answer for the next hour or so.

The downside to this little course of action was that Janelle and I ended up clearing and doing the dishes! We put in place another rule to stop this – but that's a story for another book!

There was a great TV show many years ago they made for families that were falling apart. They made them have dinner together with no phones or any distractions for 30 straight days. It was amazing how these families came back together.

my learnings:

- ☑ Clarity brings focus to my Vision and Mission
- ☑ I will move a lot of 'dirt' to get to my gold.
- ☑ I must always look toward tomorrow and plan for opportunities

Your learnings:

- ☐
- ☐
- ☐

The Landing - Final thoughts

The A380 is nearing its destination, and the pilots are getting ready to land. They have pre-set the throttles for descent and are now going through their list of pre-landing checks. The passengers are getting ready to disembark, and the flight attendants are readying the cabin for landing. Everything has been thought about and planned, and all potential issues thought about, checked and spoken about before the pilots line up to land on that runway and then taxi into the gate. Nothing is a surprise or left to chance.

Your family and your business should have the same type of checklist that pilots go through to ensure everything is functioning as it should be.

Make your cockpit so that your communication is being clear about what you want. Listening for clarification from your business colleagues and your family is also an important step. You want people in your business to know and understand what you are saying. Importantly, you also want your family to understand your message, and what you are saying.

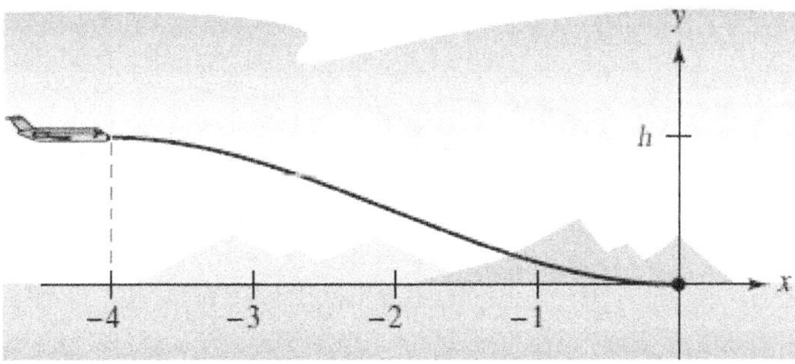

They need to be on the same glide path as you are, and you need to know that they are on that glide path. Otherwise, there's a crash-landing about to happen. This is why Communication is so important.

Most importantly like pilots having to listen to Air Traffic Control for instructions, make sure you do lots of listening as well. A great part of communication is listening for understanding.

The 'four engines' of your business and personal relationships are,

Mindset

Relationships and Business

Parenting Techniques and Business

Goal setting

These are the power platforms that will transform your business and your personal relationships. Make sure you have the correct fuel and enough of it, to power each engine, so you obtain the ultimate results you require and desire. Remember, it takes a lot of fuel and thrust to push that big aeroplane into the air. It will be the same for your relationships and your business. Don't starve them of fuel. Push the throttles up, spool those mighty engines and push forward and get the momentum going.

A thought

Just because you've landed, doesn't mean it is the end of the journey. You have reached your first destination. You are now equipped with resources and knowledge to impact the next chapter of your journey.

So go on, get off the plane, go through customs and immigration and out the door to your next venture. You have the tools and expertise to reach this next destination on your journey, quickly and effectively.

Don't wait for tomorrow to make something happen. The power to make a difference is within your grasp now.

Your family and running your business are two of the most important aspects of your life. You know now, not to listen to negative people in your life, saying you won't amount to anything. They are a drain and bring you down because they have lost their desire and are jealous in case you succeed. That is way too much power to let anyone have over you. Run, run as fast as you can away from them.

Ensure your mindset is at its very best. Just as your body needs the right food to give it the proper energy for work, your mind needs to be properly nourished as well. Equip it with good powerful thoughts. Nourish it by having positive affirmations and affirming thoughts. Remember, what you feed it, will ultimately return to you in the form you fed it but probably two-fold.

Feeding your top 2 inches with good thoughts is important. It determines your destiny. You should have a mindset that is like a cactus. It never gives up, and it never dies. You may be a minute away from success without realising it. If you give up, you'll never know.

Form great habits. If you're serious about changing your life, you must stop practicing bad habits and start instituting good ones. Start a good habit by implementing what Lee Iacocca said;

"If you can't be at home for dinner at 6:00 with your family, you're running your business wrong."

Your dream chart should be created and displayed on the wall where you can see it every day.

Remember the formula for success.

dreams x goals x learning x plans x action = success

Ensure your dream chart, has things on that are private and family oriented, as well as business goals.

Your business is there to work for you to make these private and family goals a reality. This book has been about helping you understand that family is important, just like business. Your business is the conduit for a great private and family life.

What's your actual goal? It comes down to a very simple thing. Plan it. What's the number that you're shooting for? Make sure you have clarity around this.

Take risks. Yes, you may fail. You may fail several times. But, without taking risks and trying, you will fail every time. It's like the farmer who sows his crop. A barn filled with seed doesn't produce a harvest but, if the farmer plants his seed, drought and frost and pests can wipe him out. Sowing is a risk. However, if he doesn't sow his seeds, he is guaranteed to fail. Without taking risks, you have no chance of succeeding at all.

Mitigate those risks before you act, and always obtain wise counsel first. When someone outside is asked to help and doesn't have a vested interest in the ultimate decision, it takes the emotion away from the decision and your perspective.

A final question for you

What is more important, your family or your job/business?

Hopefully, your answer is family after reading this book.

As Winston Churchill said; "*There is no doubt that it is around the family and the home that all the greatest virtues, the most dominating virtues of humans are created, strengthened and maintained*".

If family is more important, why do we spend so much time trying to get our working environment right and not as much time managing our family environment and getting it right? This book should have shifted your mindset to understand the importance of family in your life. Have the same attention to detail and professionalism that you use in your job or business?

Now you're at the end of the book, you will have a checklist of all you need to do to get your business and your relationship ready for growth.

You have flown through the turbulence of how to understand that both are intertwined. Now that the turbulence is behind you, enjoy the smooth flying of your relationship and business. You deserve it having got to your destination on the first part of your journey. Celebrate your relationship. You have a great friendship now. You've come through the turbulence to a harmonious friendship. People see the difference in you.

Celebrate your business success. You now have more money and more time. Celebrate that the business is not running you anymore, you are running it and are in control.

Lastly, may I leave you with this poem to ponder, as you move along your journey of life toward your next great achievement:

There was a very cautious man who never laughed or played

He never risked, he never tried, he never sang or prayed.

And when one day he passed away, his insurance was denied

For since he never really lived, they claimed he never died.

Remember, Family does matter, and so does Business!

My learnings:

- ☑ Winning is about having the right set of rules
- ☑ The importance of timing is paramount in anything I do
- ☑ My six core Human Needs must be met for me to grow

Your learnings:

- ☐
- ☐
- ☐

The Black Dog

It was International Suicide Prevention Week a while ago. And I was out on my walk one morning during that week, and I thought to myself, gee wiz, I've actually been on that journey through this suicide, this depression stuff, the BLACK DOG that I call it and how the BLACK DOG can really bark at you.

So, I have added an extra bonus chapter because many Business owners go through a really tough time sometimes, and unfortunately many make a wrong choice. And that moment in time, that lapse of judgement impacts immensely on the people that are left behind.

Now if you're depressed, if you're thinking of suicide, please read this chapter because I'm an example of how you can get through.

Now, this chapter is for two people here.

First one, if you're thinking of suicide, if you're depressed and you don't see a way out, then this chapter is for you.

Secondly, if you're a person and your partner is really depressed or even having those suicidal thoughts, then this chapter is for you because I want to give you a couple of tips as to how to get through, because you're going through the 'hell' of it with your partner and sometimes you just have no idea what to do. And again, I say to you I'm lucky. I'm the living example that I have got through, so you and your partner can as well – even though it will be a tough tough journey.

4 really important words, THIS TOO WILL PASS – I PROMISE you it will, if you take on board the learnings I'm offering here.

Now the main thing is, I'm not a well-known person. I'm not a superstar or a star. We hear these people in the world that are the superstars that have gone through this and you think, oh yeah, it's OK for them. They're rich, they'll get through.

But we very rarely hear from just ordinary people that are working and living life, just like you and I.

I want you to understand the journey that I've been on…and that you will come out the other side. I PROMISE you; you will come out the other side if you look at some of these tips that I am going to give you, and implement them.

It's a little bit embarrassing telling my story, but if it can help someone think, "oh gee, someone else just like me has gone through this, someone who is really similar to me and they got through this," then it will be worthwhile.

Back in 2018, 2019, I had Major League depression. Now I'm saying, Major League, like the American baseball Major Leagues!

I was working in a franchise at that stage and it was absolutely, literally killing me.

It was just one of the worst times in my life that I have ever gone through. I couldn't get out of bed in the morning. I really struggled to get out of bed. In fact, sometimes I would just lie in bed and say, "I'll just have another five minutes." And then after five minutes I'd say, "I need just another five minutes". And I could stay in bed for an hour-and-a-half, two hours, just going through all those five minutes, one after the other. And let me tell you, it wasn't doing me any good.

So, the thing is that when I was going through my "Black Dog" stage, I couldn't get out of bed. I didn't want to go to work. I didn't want to see people. And the business was starting to implode at this stage. I had all the pressures coming down on me that I felt, I'm not working, - business isn't going to work.

And I'll tell you what, my wife, she was also struggling, because of what I was going through. I'm going to talk about this fairly soon because the partners of people who are going through depression and suicide, they also struggle a hell of a lot as well. And my wife, she just didn't know what to do at this stage because of where I was at.

So, Janelle and I, we had a chat one day and I said, "I've got to get out of this Franchise, because if I don't, I'm gonna die, quite literally." And we had a very frank and open discussion. Something had to change. We made the decision to remove ourselves from that Franchise that was literally killing me. And I'll tell you what, once I'd made that decision to get out of my current situation, then all of a sudden, the pressure started to come off. Getting out of that particular Franchise was the best thing I ever did because if I didn't, I wouldn't have been able to write this particular chapter.

The Black Dog

Because at that stage, I was actually living day to day. And it got to the stage where I got down to living hour to hour. I would just try and make it through the next hour. And blinking heck, that was tough. And I tell you what, I started to contemplate suicide. That's how bad it got. And for me to look back now, thinking that, I thought, man oh man, that's a bad place to be. Me of all people, who was big and strong and done some wild things in my life. I don't know whether I could have carried anything out to harm myself or not, but the thoughts were there. And I realized that I needed to get help.

And it's when I got help and got out of that Franchise that things started to come right. But only because I had help from outside sources. I actually reached out for help, because I realised, I couldn't do it by myself. And I had to humble myself to go to people and say, "I need help." And I went to my doctor. And I hounded my doctor to give me the right pills to try and help me get out from my depression, from my suicidal thoughts. And it took me 4 different sets of pills before I found the right ones for me.

And sitting here again, now I've got to say to you that four little words that I remember that I kept on saying to myself is that THIS TOO WILL PASS. So, if you're going through a dark stage, and you can hear the BLACK DOG barking, then remember, THIS TOO

WILL PASS. You can come out the other side of this, and I'll tell you what, it is a great place to be.

Now going through depression and having suicidal thoughts, it's just awful, and I get that because I've been there. And as I said, when I was just living hour to hour, what I would do is, I would say, "when I get to the end of this hour, I'm gonna give myself a little reward." And it might be where I'd go and have a cup of coffee, a really nice cup of coffee. Or it just could be, "I'll have just something really nice to eat," for example. But I had to reward myself to get through that hour, and get through that day. Sometimes I'd go into town and I'd just sit and watch people and have a coffee. And I'll tell you what, I didn't want to talk to anyone. If someone came up to talk to me, I go, "oh no, go away." Because I became really introverted, and didn't want to talk with anyone. But it was just nice to get out and be in the fresh air.

And the other thing that I found really helpful, was exercise. Every day I made myself, quite literally made myself go and exercise. And if you know me, I've always been one where I've enjoyed my running, my walking, my hiking, but I really struggled to get out of bed, as I said, and go and exercise, but it did help. It really helped. I never pushed myself to run or walk a particular distance, or at a particular pace. I just went out for an hour and walked or ran. It was being out and just exercising – doing something that helped.

If you're going through a BLACK DOG stage, then exercise will really help on two fronts. Your mental capacity will improve and your cardiovascular will also benefit from just getting out and exercising. Even if it's only for 10 minutes to start with – I PROMISE you, it will help

The Black Dog

As I said, I reached out for help. I didn't like it. I didn't want to do that because I felt that I wasn't a strong person by reaching out for help. I wasn't a man anymore. If you're feeling like that, forget those silly, silly thoughts, because you're more of a person, when you reach out for help than not asking for help at all. Let me say that again - you're more of a person, when you reach out for help than not asking for help at all.

If I can say also, if you're a partner of someone going through this, then you've got to look after yourself as well, because it is really tough on you when you've got your partner who is going through big depression. You must look after yourself so please reach out for help for yourself so you can get help with what you're going through. Because it is blinking tough, and I know that for a fact. If you're not OK, then you're not in a position to help your partner properly come out from under where they are and stop that BLACK DOG barking at them.

An army will normally attack just before dawn, because that's when it's darkest. And I'll tell you, when you're going through depression and suicide, it can be that dark – very dark. Being in the darkest hour before dawn, wondering, "can I get out of this?" Where's the attack coming from? And that BLACK DOG that sits on your shoulder and barks, you've just got to wrestle with it. You've really got to wrestle with it and try and be stronger, and push through. But with the help of other people, other people you can lean on to guide you through this dark place, you will get through. I PROMISE you that.

Now, the thing is that I didn't ask for help to start with, because I was trying to look after my own sanity, thinking, "no, I'll be able to tough this out." That was one of the stupidest thoughts I ever had. And I know when you're in there, in that dark place, you don't want to ask for help, but I'm saying to you now, PLEASE do.

The Black Dog

If you're a partner of someone going through this depression, the suicide, then just take the bull by the horns and seek help for them – and you. Ask for help for them. The person may not like it at the time, but I guarantee you they will thank you for it later on. Absolutely they will thank you for it later on. Because if in the moment they have a small lapse of judgement it has huge ramifications on everyone left behind. And on yourself because you will wonder 'What if.' What if I'd asked for, or got help, would my partner still be here today? No-one wants that 'What if' feeling. So be strong and get help for your partner – regardless of what they are saying to you.

Do it right now. And if you're in that dark place remember if you do anything silly by taking your own life then you won't have the opportunity to live a life that is fun, that you can be proud of, - if you take your own life.

Now, when I reached out for help, I'm gonna be quite honest here, I had my God there as well. I prayed fervently day after day after day. And I'll tell you, with my God and with the counsellors, that helped me to get through, I came out the other side. To be honest it was touch and go there for a while! And yes, God and the counsellors were a crutch. I put my hand up to that. I needed that crutch to lean on and in my God and the counsellors I had that. And being dependent on them got me through.

Now, the thing is that, what I need to tell you is that I went through 4 counsellors before I found the right one. So please, if you go to a counsellor and they're not the right one, that's no reflection on them, and it's no reflection on you either. It just isn't the right fit and that's OK. So, please keep going to the counsellors until you find the right one that's gonna help you.

And I'm going to tell you right now that I found a counsellor in Faversham here, and I've got to tell you her name, Jan Williams. She is the most amazing person. And funnily enough, for me, I didn't think I'd be able to utilize a woman because I thought I'm too much of a man's man. How silly of me. Jan was absolutely brilliant. And if I can, I would love to recommend Jan to you. Her handle is The Change Within. Look her up. If you are having some issues, talk to Jan, and she will be able to help you to!

And through my Bible readings also, I realized, I'm not the only one that's going through this because Elijah also had Major League depression. He actually asked God, "end my life!" Now that's really Major League Depression. So, I realized that there's been people throughout history that have had the same issues that I've had, that you are possibly having. And they've got through, so I realised I can get through as well.

Now in fairness, I'd had depression back in 2006. I'd done this marathon run and I'd run so fast and hard that I ran myself into the ground and I was hospitalized in intensive care for five days. My enzymes levels had just gone through the roof because I had Rhabdomyolysis.

And then I had another bout of depression in 2008 when my marriage blew apart, and that was also another major time, but nothing suicidal. It wasn't until 2018, 2019 when I was in that Franchise that the major league stuff really hit me and the suicidal thoughts actually manifested themselves and I was in a really really bad way.

The Black Dog

And I'll tell you, I had a second set of counsellors helping me through as well. The mental health counsellors in Canterbury were also amazing. And they'd just set up a brand-new system where, there'll be two ladies come and they spoke with me. And it was funny because I'd be talking with them, and then they'd talk to each other, about me. And I thought, what the hell is going on here? I would say, "hey guys, I'm in the room here. You can talk to me!" And they had to explain to me that what they do is they talk around me, about me, to me to actually, to give me the appropriate advice that I needed. And it went really well. So, I was working with two sets of counsellors. Jan and the Crisis team.

I didn't have the right medication that I needed either. And I went through things like citalopram, escitalopram, and fluoxetine which can be prescribed by a doctor. But when I was talking with the Canterbury Crisis team, they actually brought a psychologist along and she was able to prescribe some Brintellix, which I now have. I don't know if I still need them, but I'm still using them because I don't want that BLACK DOG sitting back on my shoulder, barking again.

And I realize now that every day, is a blessing, and it's great to be here, but I keep saying to myself, THIS TOO WILL PASS. And always remember that as your mantra.

If I can say again just to your partner, if you've got your partner going through this really tough time, then you're going through it as well. So, you've got to look after yourself and go and get some counselling or some help for yourself to make sure that you can get through it to help them, because you're no good if you fall down as well. So, don't be scared to do that yourself. Reach out for help because people do want to help.

And here's the crazy thing about it. Jan Williams, my counsellor said this to me. She said, "you know, if someone came to you and they reached out for help, would you help them?" I said, "yeah, of course I would. I'd be more than happy to". And she said to me, and this really, really resonated with me. She said, "well, why don't you think people want to help you?" And I sat back and I thought, that is just so right, isn't it? That is just so right. So again, I've reached out for help and doing this chapter is somewhat embarrassing. I've got to admit that. But I want to do it because if my fights with the BLACK DOG, as I call it, can move me through the tough tough stages, then you can too! The depression and that suicide. And if I can help you to get through your issues, it's going be great.

I'm now really relaxed and happy with life. Have I beaten the BLACK DOG? To a certain extent, yes, but I know that he's always there ready to bark. He's there slinking in the background, slinking around on his belly, ready to bark again, so I have to eyeball him, and call him out, so I don't regress again. And I've got to ensure that I don't give him that opportunity, by not feeding him. So, I do my affirmations. Every day I do my affirmations. I'm thinking good thoughts, because I know the mindset, my top 2 inches, is the most important part to beating the BLACK DOG.

The Black Dog

So, when you're getting counselling, also look at your affirmations. And I've got 3 affirmations that I say to myself every day. When I was going through my really tough patches, I was probably saying these affirmations eight, nine, ten times a day. Just putting the good thoughts into my life, and into my head. And may I tell you, they really help because the subconscious doesn't know right from wrong. So, what you feed it, it's going to go to work to help you, because it thinks, that's important. So, if you're going to feed yourself negative stuff, your mind's going to work to make that happen. DON'T. Feed yourself and your mind positive stuff. Affirmations are also a really really important part of beating the BLACK DOG.

The counselling I had, has given me the skills and the processes to continue on, to keep going and not allow the BLACK DOG to bark and derail me. And can I say, if you're contemplating suicide, **PLEASE DON'T**. Please don't go there, because it's one momentary lapse in time and that's all it is, one momentary lapse that has huge repercussions for the rest, well not your life as such, but your family, your friends, your partner, who are all left behind. All those people left behind. It has huge repercussions on them. So, if you're thinking of it, **please don't**.

Go out now and get help because that momentary lapse has such a huge impact, not on you only, but on your family and your friends. So, I've got to say it again, **please don't**. And remember those four words, THIS TOO, WILL PASS. Because in an hour when you get through this and you think, oh thank goodness I didn't do that. And I'm talking from experience where I had to go through hour to hour to get me through.

I read somewhere that high-performing people are susceptible to depression. Now I've never really thought of myself as a high-performing person, but I kind of think maybe I am, with what I have been through. So, if you're there and you're depressed, it could be because you're a high-performing person, is what I read.

Now, when you get through the moment, as I said, right at the start, I PROMISE you, it will be worth it. I PROMISE you it will be worth getting through that moment in time to be with your friends, to be with your family, to do the things you enjoy in life, like seeing sunrises and sunsets, maybe enjoying a nice glass of cold beer on a warm day, or a lovely glass of wine as you sit and talk with your partner or friends.

Don't do anything stupid because it's the worst thing you can ever do.

I'm over a year now, away from having the BLACK DOG, wag its tail at me and barking. One year getting out of the depression loop and you know what – it feels fabulous to still be alive and smelling life, seeing the blue sky, getting rained on, and just being alive.

The Black Dog

And one of the things that really helped me, and this is where I got more help as well, because a friend of mine, when I got out of the Franchise, offered me a job to come and work in his business. And I'll tell you, it was one of the most wonderful, wonderful offers I've ever had in my life. And that's another reason why I'm here, because I didn't want to let him down because he'd given me such a wonderful offer.

And going there and learning from him and then just doing something different and then implementing some of the stuff he was telling me and showing me, I thought, wow, I wish I'd known about this before. Before I had to go through all this rubbish that I went through.

Now here's the thing, and here's something interesting. Sometimes we have to go through this stuff. There's a reason for it. We may not know it at the time. But when we come out the other side, we actually get great learnings and realise, hey, this was the learning. This is the reason that I had to go through this stuff. And please believe me on this, I never want to go through that crap again. And neither does my wife and I don't want to put her through that again. I don't want to put her through that, ever again.

So, we talk about it and I'm actually happy to go and talk with people about it as well. So please, if you feel as though you can't take any more, you can't get through this, please reach out for help. Don't wait.

If you're the partner of someone going through depression, and I'll say it again, go and get the help for yourself and for your partner who's feeling depressed or suicidal. They are going to thank you for it in the long run, it's worthwhile. In the short term, it's blinking difficult.

I'll say it again, get through the moment now, because I PROMISE you it will be okay in the end. I PROMISE you that.

Look, that's just my story. It's been a tough one, but if it can help you, then reach out for help, go and talk to someone and be humble. Be humble to do the things so that you don't end up as one of those statistics that we don't want to read about or hear about. I'm Pete. That's my story. Please take care. Look after yourself. Be careful. Be happy. Look after yourself and look after your family, your friends, because you and they will be the poorer for it if something happens to you.

The Black Dog

APPENDIX

Incantation Sheet

This was given to me by Tosin Ogunnusi of **Mpowerment** and has had a profound effect in my life. I reproduce it and say thanks to Tosin.

His website can be found at

Tosin Ogunnusi: https://mpowerment.co.uk/about/

CREATE YOUR NEW IDENTITY
Sheet 1 - Adjectives

Tick between three and five of the words below - the words that jump out to you the most…

- [ ] Adorable
- [ ] Adventurous
- [ ] Aggressive
- [ ] Alert
- [ ] Amazing
- [ ] Articulate
- [ ] Attractive
- [ ] Awesome
- [ ] Beautiful
- [ ] Breathtaking
- [ ] Bright
- [ ] Brilliant
- [ ] Caring
- [ ] Cheeky
- [ ] Childlike
- [ ] Clean
- [ ] Clear
- [ ] Colourful
- [ ] Confident
- [ ] Courageous
- [ ] Creative
- [ ] Curious
- [ ] Cute
- [ ] Elegant
- [ ] Energetic
- [ ] Exciting
- [ ] Fabulous
- [ ] Faithful
- [ ] Fancy
- [ ] Famboyant
- [ ] Flexible
- [ ] Flirty
- [ ] Fulfilled
- [ ] Funny
- [ ] Graceful
- [ ] Grateful
- [ ] Handsome
- [ ] Happy
- [ ] Humorous
- [ ] Inspiring
- [ ] Intelligent
- [ ] Joyful
- [ ] Kind
- [ ] Light
- [ ] Loving
- [ ] Loyal
- [ ] Magnificent
- [ ] Outstanding
- [ ] Plain
- [ ] Playful
- [ ] Positive
- [ ] Powerful
- [ ] Powerful
- [ ] Precious
- [ ] Sexy
- [ ] Shiny
- [ ] Sincere
- [ ] Sparkling
- [ ] Spectacular
- [ ] Spotless
- [ ] Trustworthy
- [ ] Unique
- [ ] Wicked
- [ ] Wonderful

CREATE YOUR NEW IDENTITY
Sheet 2 - Nouns

Tick between three and five of the words or phrases below - the ones that jump out to you the most...

- ☐ Achiever
- ☐ Angel
- ☐ Author
- ☐ Authority
- ☐ Billionaire
- ☐ Catalyst
- ☐ Cause
- ☐ Champion
- ☐ Coach
- ☐ Comedian
- ☐ Commander
- ☐ Creator
- ☐ Dancer
- ☐ Destiny forger
- ☐ Director
- ☐ Earth
- ☐ Expression of health
- ☐ Family
- ☐ Father
- ☐ God
- ☐ Goddess
- ☐ Grandfather
- ☐ Grandmother
- ☐ Guru
- ☐ Healer
- ☐ Heart
- ☐ Instrument
- ☐ Kiss
- ☐ Leader
- ☐ Legend
- ☐ Man
- ☐ Manager
- ☐ Mverick
- ☐ Memory
- ☐ Mentor
- ☐ Millionaire
- ☐ Mother
- ☐ Mother nature
- ☐ Motivator
- ☐ Mountain
- ☐ Musician
- ☐ Ocean
- ☐ Oneness
- ☐ Orator
- ☐ Playground
- ☐ Prince
- ☐ Princess
- ☐ Professional
- ☐ Professor
- ☐ Representative
- ☐ Role model
- ☐ Sculpture of souls
- ☐ Sex machine
- ☐ Spark
- ☐ Star
- ☐ Student
- ☐ Summer
- ☐ Supermodel
- ☐ Superstar
- ☐ Teacher
- ☐ Team
- ☐ Tiger
- ☐ Universe
- ☐ Voice
- ☐ Woman

CREATE YOUR NEW IDENTITY
Sheet 3 - Verbs

Tick between three and five of the words below - the ones that jump out to you the most...

- ☐ Accelerates
- ☐ Activates
- ☐ Administers
- ☐ Advises
- ☐ Amuses
- ☐ Analyses
- ☐ Anticipates
- ☐ Appreciates
- ☐ Arranges
- ☐ Creates
- ☐ Creates opportunities
- ☐ Delivers high standards
- ☐ Demonstrates
- ☐ Develops
- ☐ Discovers others
- ☐ Elevates others
- ☐ Encourages
- ☐ Entertains
- ☐ Experiments
- ☐ Feeds
- ☐ Focussed
- ☐ Gathers information
- ☐ Grabs opportunities
- ☐ Guides
- ☐ Heals people
- ☐ Inspires Light
- ☐ Inspires others to do more
- ☐ Investigates
- ☐ Leads
- ☐ Lights the next torch
- ☐ Loves
- ☐ Maintains
- ☐ Makes a difference
- ☐ Makes dreams come true
- ☐ Makes the word a better place
- ☐ Motivates others
- ☐ Opens doors
- ☐ Persuades
- ☐ Plays full out
- ☐ Powerful
- ☐ Protects others
- ☐ Provides
- ☐ Recommends
- ☐ Reorganises
- ☐ Rocks
- ☐ Runs
- ☐ Saves the planet
- ☐ Shares
- ☐ Spreads
- ☐ Stimulates
- ☐ Strengthens
- ☐ Stretches
- ☐ Succeeds
- ☐ Supplies
- ☐ Supports others
- ☐ Sybolises
- ☐ Systemises
- ☐ Takes ownership
- ☐ Takes responsibility
- ☐ Taps into potential
- ☐ Travels
- ☐ Understands
- ☐ Unlocks
- ☐ Upgrades
- ☐ Utilises

CREATE YOUR NEW IDENTITY
Sheet 4 - My New Identity

Now it's time to create your new identity from the words you have chosen. We do this by writing them out as follows:

I (your name) am (list your adjectives here) and (list nouns here) that (list verbs here)

For example:

"I Pete O'Keeffe am Adventurous, Courageous, Inspiring, Kind, Powerful, Positive and Trustworthy, and I'm an Achiever, a Commander, a Leader a Maverick, a Father and someone who must have God in his life, who creates opportunities for others, protects others, encourages, supports and inspires, and takes responsibility to make a difference in the world, so it becomes a better place"

Now it's your turn:

I ____________________ am ______________________________

____

and ____

____

____

that ____

____

____

This is your new identity - Say it with pride!

TAKE ACTION

Be the person you want to be. To really feel the benefits of your new identity, say it out load to yourself in the mirror EVERY day for 90 days.

YOUR 12 MONTH GOAL SHEET - *BUSINESS*

"To begin with the end in mind means to start with a clear understanding of your destination. It means to know where you're going so that you better understand where you are now and so that the steps you take are always in the right direction." Steven R. Covey

Name: ________________ Business: ________________

GOAL	WHY ?	WHAT DO I HAVE TO DO TO ACHIEVE THE GOAL?	WHO DO I HAVE TO BE TO GET THERE?
1. 2.			
3. 4.			

Signed: Date:

YOUR 12 MONTH GOAL SHEET - *PERSONAL*

"To begin with the end in mind means to start with a clear understanding of your destination. It means to know where you're going so that you better understand where you are now and so that the steps you take are always in the right direction." Steven R. Covey

Name: ________________ Business: ________________

GOAL	WHY ?	WHAT DO I HAVE TO DO TO ACHIEVE THE GOAL?	WHO DO I HAVE TO BE TO GET THERE?
1. 2.			
3. 4.			

Signed: Date:

BUSINESS PLANNING

Strategies	1	2	3	4	5	6	7	8	9	10	11	12	13
Events...													
Study...													

If you would like to contact Pete, with any thoughts, suggestions, or questions, then please go to:

www.globalbizsuccess.com

or

e-mail: **pete@globalbizsuccess.com**

He will welcome any correspondence that is sent.

Pete and Janelle run Leadership training programmes for CEO's and their staff. Either in house or on-line

They will also run Staff Engagements programmes that ensures staff are happier and more productive. These also are in-house or on-line

Allied to these are bespoke:

Transformation days,
Workshops,
Bootcamps
Retreats for Business owners and their Teams

If you would like to know, please email Janelle at **janelle@globalbizsuccess.com**

ABOUT THE AUTHOR

Pete was born in Perth, Australia, grew up in Hamilton, New Zealand, attended Sacred Heart Boarding College in Auckland, NZ and worked in the Police for 18 years in South Auckland and Blenheim. He started his first business at the age of 40 and ran another two, before moving to England and starting another business there.

Having been involved in four business start-ups, Pete understands the difficulties of maintaining a business and a functioning family amidst the 'noise and clutter' that dominate our lives today. Pete certainly made a hash of both his businesses and family at various times. Having realised his mistakes (and good points), he brings a clarity and understanding of how to keep both in perspective.

This book is a culmination of Pete's life learnings on running a business and a family at the same time. It is written unequivocally from a man's perspective and looks at how our emotions or lack of them, can affect both family and business. It is raw at times and emotional but brutally honest.

If this book keeps just one business running as opposed to ending in financial ruin, or keeps one family together and intact, then it will have served its purpose.

Family does matter – and so does Business!

Printed in Great Britain
by Amazon

55677428R00149